iConquer Speech Anxiety

A Workbook to Help You Overcome Your Nervousness & Anxiety about Public Speaking

KAREN KANGAS DWYER, PHD

PREFACE

IConquer Speech Anxiety is written for anyone else who wants to overcome the nervousness and anxiety of public speaking. For over twenty years, I have researched communication apprehension, taught university students and workshop participants how to overcome excessive nervousness about speaking in public. This is the result of those efforts.

IConquer Speech Anxiety presents a unique multidimensional approach that will help you pinpoint the source of your speech anxiety and then develop a plan to fit your personality. This book also presents a combination of research-based techniques for overcoming speech anxiety in a user-friendly program. Several years of communication research will attest to the workable success of this combinational approach. Countless numbers of my students and workshop participants can testify that this multidimensional program has given them (as it will give you) a new confidence to speak in public and change your life.

This book is not meant to completely replace a public speaking textbook, course or club; public speaking skills are only covered in a brief overview to give the reader a starting point for understanding basic skills. If in fact you are reading this book on your own, as soon as you are finished, you should try to enroll in a public speaking course, workshop, or public speaking club/organization where you can learn and practice public speaking skills. The confidence in public speaking that you are seeking will be acquired by using the speech anxiety– reduction techniques presented here in concert with practicing public speaking skills under the instruction of a communication teacher or coach or mentor.

PART 1, "Understanding Speech Anxiety," will help you learn the definition, possible causes, and impact public speaking anxiety has or can have on your life.

Chapter One, "Speech Anxiety and You," points out that speech anxiety is a common anxiety which takes commitment to conquer. In this chapter, you will assess your commitment to overcoming it, and write a pledge to yourself summarizing your willingness to practice the anxiety reduction techniques.

Chapter Two, "Definitions and Assessments," discusses communication apprehension, one of the academic terms for speech anxiety. It explains the four types of communication apprehension and guides you in assessing your level and type of communication anxiety.

Chapter Three, "Causes of Speech Anxiety," outlines several causes of communication anxiety to help you understand your experience. You will also learn that it does not matter how or when you acquired your anxious feelings about public communication; the techniques presented in this book will help you overcome it.

Chapter Four, "Excessive Activation and the Fight-Flight-Freeze Response," explains the fight or flight or freeze response, the source of your aggravating physical sensations associated with an anxiety and nervousness about public speaking. You will assess your symptoms of excessive activation and learn how to stop the fight-flight-freeze response.

PART 2, "Treating Speech Anxiety," presents the multidimensional approach to alleviating speech anxiety. It discusses how to apply each of the speech anxiety–reduction techniques and contains seven chapters.

Chapter Five, "A Multidimensional Plan for Conquering Speech Anxiety" explains the multidimensional approach and how to pinpoint the source of your speech anxiety as the place to begin treatment. You will determine your "firing order" of personality dimensions using the "BASICS" evaluation guide, and then choose techniques that match your personality dimensions to create a personalized plan for conquering your speech anxiety.

Chapter Six, "Diaphragmatic Breathing," presents deep breathing exercises in order to induce relaxation and reduce stress. The three-minute, diaphragmatic breathing exercise provides a quick fix that brings on relaxation and is an essential part of other speech anxiety– reduction techniques. It targets the affect and sensation personality dimensions. You will evaluate your own breathing, and then practice deep breathing exercises.

Chapter Seven, "Cognitive Restructuring," explains the four steps in this rational technique to disengage your irrational, anxious beliefs about public speaking. It targets your cognitive personality dimension. You will make a list of your worries about public speaking, identify the irrational beliefs and distortions, create a new list of positive coping statements, and then practice your coping statements until they replace your old, anxious beliefs.

Chapter Eight, "Systematic Desensitization," presents the three steps in this technique that help alleviate a learned nervousness response to speaking in public. The affect, sensation, and imagery personality dimensions are targeted. You will develop a hierarchy about anxious events in public speaking, learn progressive muscle relaxation, and then condition relaxation in association with the events on your hierarchy.

Chapter Nine, "Mental Rehearsal (Visualization)," teaches you how to rehearse a successful speech in your mind before you present it. It targets the cognitive and imagery personality dimensions and thus helps reduce anxiety by preparing your mind for a positive communication experience. You will practice mental rehearsal to prepare for a speech just as many athletes do to prepare for a sporting event.

Chapter Ten, "Physical Exercise and Interpersonal Support" discusses the importance of incorporating regular exercise and social support into your personal plan to reduce speech anxiety. Physical exercise targets stress (drugs/biological personality dimension) and helps reduce tension in general, as well as public speaking anxiety. Social support also targets stress (interpersonal relationships personality dimension) by buffering the impact of stress and supporting you in your goal of conquering speech anxiety.

Chapter Eleven, "Skills Training" targets the behavior personality dimension and helps build confidence and competence in public speaking. In this chapter, you will complete a public speaking skills checklist and learn about some of the essential public speaking skills.

PART 3, "Putting It All Together," explains how to put together all that you have learned into a personal plan targeted to your needs.

Chapter Twelve, "Putting It All Together to Conquer Speech Anxiety," summarizes the plan you will follow to conquer your speech anxiety. You need to commit yourself to the goal of conquering speech anxiety, actively learn the techniques, follow your personal plan, and participate in public communication.

SUPPLEMENTAL MATERIALS

In addition to the book, four iConquer Speech Anxiety MP3 files are available to help you learn and practice the speech anxiety–reduction techniques (see www.iconquerspeechanxiety.com). The files explain the state-of-the-art, research-proven techniques for overcoming speech anxiety. The techniques are described in detail so you can learn them by diligent practice with each recording, during a time that is most convenient for you. The speech anxiety–alleviation techniques on the MP3 files include: 1) cognitive restructuring, 2) diaphragmatic breathing exercises, 3) systematic desensitization (with deep muscle relaxation), and 4) mental rehearsal (also called visualization).

An instructor's manual, written by the author, is also available for instructors upon request to the author. The manual includes unit and course outlines, lesson plans, exercises, assignments, and suggested readings.

CONTENTS

PART ONE: SPEECH ANXIETY & YOU
CHAPTER ONE
SPEECH ANXIETY AND YOU

Congratulations!

You have now made one of the best decisions of your life. You have decided to take action to conquer your speech anxiety. This decision is the first step in getting rid of all those nervous feelings, sensations, and negative thoughts about public speaking. This book will give you the skills you need to help you achieve your goal. **YOU CAN CONQUER SPEECH ANXIETY and BECOME A COMPETENT AND CONFIDENT SPEAKER.**

1.1 The Truth about Speech Anxiety

You may think you are the ONLY ONE who experiences anxiety related to public speaking. The truth is YOU HAVE A LOT OF COMPANY. In fact, surveys involving thousands of college students and adults indicate that between 60 to 75 percent of our population reports a fear or anxiety about public speaking.[1] In other words, almost three out of every four people you meet would say they have a fear or anxiety when it comes to speaking in front of others.

> **Shelby (photographer), age 22,** said: "I thought I was the only one who has ever dreaded giving a speech. In fact, I thought my anxious feelings and fearful thoughts about giving a speech was a problem that no one else had ever experienced…. What a relief to know that many people had this same anxiety and have conquered it. This will open all new career opportunities for me."

1.2 The Fear of Public Speaking is a Common Fear

The Bruskin Report lists the fear of public speaking as the most selected "common fear" in America, even above the fear of heights, bugs, financial problems, deep water, sickness, and DEATH.[2] In fact, when 2543 adult Americans were asked to pick items from a list representing situations in which they had some degree of fear, 41 percent selected speaking before a group, while only 19 percent selected death.[3] A recent fears study asking the same question of college students found that 62% selected speaking before a group, while 55% listed financial problems, and 42% listed death.[4] So if you thought you were alone in your fear or anxiety about public speaking, now you know that a majority of those around you also experience public speaking anxiety. However, there is one thing that makes you different from the others: **YOU have made the decision to conquer your anxiety.**

1.3 A Good First Step

In the past, you may have hoped your fear or nervousness about public speaking would miraculously disappear. When it did not, you may have felt your speech anxiety was hopeless and you should simply try to avoid speaking in front of a group. However, you soon discovered you could not avoid public communication and still accomplish your personal goals in life. So you purchased this book in an effort to help you surmount the problem.

Actively reading this book, completing the exercises, and practicing the techniques **WILL HELP YOU.** No matter how long you have had an anxiety about public speaking, no matter how intense your nervousness has become, and no matter where your public speaking anxiety originated, YOU CAN OVERCOME IT. The techniques presented in this book are supported by more than sixty years of communication research involving numerous communication scholars, educators, and counselors. They have helped thousands of people of all ages manage their fear, anxiety, and nervousness about public speaking. So be assured; you have taken the first step toward conquering your anxiety.

> **Tim (computer hardware engineer), age 23,** had tried everything he could to avoid speaking in front of others. "In college, I offered to write a 25-page paper in lieu of giving a speech for a class assignment. In job interviews, I would skip going if I found it involved a group of interviewers. If I had to speak in front of others on my job, I kept making excuses or pleaded illness. (Once, I really did get sick thinking about giving a speech.) Although I was able to avoid public speaking in high school, in college it became increasingly difficult to avoid--it affected my grades. In my job as a computer hardware engineer, it kept me from reaching my goals…I decided to conquer this nervousness. . . . It's one of the best things I've ever done. The speech anxiety–reduction techniques really work."

1.4 The Four Keys to Success

Have you ever learned to play a new sport or speak a new language? If so, you will remember that it took special effort, focus and commitment. Learning to overcome speech anxiety will require similar effort, commitment, practice, and participation--these are the four keys to successfully defeat speech anxiety.

For example, consider an athletic sport that you enjoy and have learned to do well. At first, you probably watched the game, tried it out, and made an effort to learn new techniques and skills. It took effort and persistence on your part. You may have sought other players to help you learn the sport, or a coach who could guide you in improving your game. You made a commitment to practice and may have even followed a practice schedule. You participated in the game at every opportunity. After a lot of practice, you learned to use your new skills and became an even better player.

Using the same keys that helped you learn a new sport or language, you can learn to overcome your nervousness about public speaking. You will need to make a commitment to put forth time and energy. This will include actively learning the techniques suggested in this book. You cannot be passive and succeed. First, you will read about the techniques, complete the exercises or journal about your progress. Next, you will take time to diligently practice the steps and plan a practice schedule. Finally, you will begin to participate by speaking before a group. You will start by delivering short speeches so you can put your knowledge and the techniques to use, while developing public speaking skills.

If you are committed to overcoming your speech anxiety; if you get actively involved in learning and doing the exercises presented here; and if you whole-heartedly practice the anxiety-reduction techniques in preparation for giving a short speech; you will become a calm and even confident speaker. Remember, athletes learn their skill not only by passively watching and practicing techniques, but most importantly by participating in the game itself. You, too, must become an active participant in learning to overcome your speech anxiety and practicing the skills.

Exercise 1.4: Your Commitment

Name   Date

Before you read any further, please have a pencil or pen in hand so you can write out answers to the following questions OR record your answers in a journal---see the following page.

1. Have you ever accomplished something in your life that took a lot of time and practice? Was your accomplishment worth your effort?

2. Describe how you see yourself as a communicator today. In everyday conversations? In group discussions? In meetings? In public speaking opportunities? Overall (in most situations)?

3. Describe your willingness to diligently practice the techniques necessary for conquering speech anxiety because practicing the techniques is essential to reducing your nervousness.

4. How much time and effort are you willing to spend to overcome your speech anxiety (e.g., one hour per day, three hours per week)?

5. Based on your answers to these questions, please write a pledge to yourself that summarizes your commitment to conquering speech anxiety and your willingness to practice the techniques presented in this book.

6. Sign and date this contract with yourself.

Signature _____**Date** _____

(TEAR-OUT PAGE FOR PRACTICE AND STUDY)

Keeping a Journal

Name   **Date**

Today, begin to keep a record of your journey toward conquering your speech anxiety. This is very helpful and you will become pleasantly surprised at your progress. Journaling will allow you to record your reactions to the anxiety-reduction techniques and evaluate your own progress over time by reviewing your journal entries. Every exercise will be followed by a journaling activity. You can choose to answer the exercise questions in this book or in your journal. If you choose to journal (a simple notebook set aside for journaling will do), you should write a few paragraphs in your journal for every exercise and every time you learn or practice a technique. If you are learning to conquer your speech anxiety through a class or workshop, record your reactions to every anxiety- reduction activity you practice. Each journal entry should include the following information:

1. **Description of the Exercise, Technique and Activity:**

2. **Practical Application Comment:** Do you understand the technique? Do you think it could help reduce your speech anxiety if you practice it more?

3. **Explain the Change in Your Anxiety Level:** Are you experiencing any alleviation of your anxiety level? How are you feeling about speaking in public now?

4. **Suggestions for Future Use:** Include any suggestions for future or alternative uses of the technique.

Journaling #1 Activity: How See Myself as a Communicator

Name   Date

Today, begin writing in your journal. Start with an assessment of how you see yourself as a communicator on this day. By journaling, you will be able to review and keep track of your progress over time.

1. Describe how you see yourself as a "communicator" today in the following situations:

   a. In everyday conversations:

   b. In group discussions or class:

   c. In meetings:

   d. In public speaking opportunities:

   e. Overall (in most situations):

2. Please describe how you experience anxiety about public speaking (stomach butterflies, racing heart, sweating, blushing, shaking limbs, shivering, feelings of panic or doom, forgetting important points, thinking worrisome or negative thoughts, etc.). Which sensations would you especially like to conquer?

3. Journal your answers to Exercise #1.3.

(BACK OF TEAR-OUT PAGE FOR PRACTICE AND STUDY)

Chapter Summary

Deciding to take action to conquer your speech anxiety is the first step in overcoming it. This book will give you the guidance you need to reach your goal. You now know you are not alone in your anxiety about public speaking; approximately three out of every four people you could meet will report a fear, anxiety, or nervousness about speaking in front of a group. Learning to overcome speech anxiety is like learning a new sport or language. The important keys to your success include effort, commitment, practice, and participation. If you make the effort and are committed to conquering speech anxiety; if you get actively involved in reading, learning, and doing the exercises or journaling; if you practice the anxiety-reduction techniques; and then if you participate in public speaking opportunities, **YOU WILL BECOME A CONFIDENT SPEAKER.**

Review Questions

After reading this chapter, you should be able to answer the following:

1. When people are asked to list their common fears or anxieties, what do they often list?

2. How many years have communication educators spent researching how to help people overcome their fear and anxiety about public speaking?

3. Learning to conquer speech anxiety can be compared to learning what other activities?

4. What challenging activities or hardships in your life have you conquered?

5. How can conquering speech anxiety be compared to learning a new language or sport?

6. What are the four keys to conquering anxiety about public speaking?

7. Which do you think will be the hardest for you to do? Why?

8. Who do you identify with most in this chapter, Shelby or Tim? Why?

Notes

[1] McCroskey, 2000; Richmond & McCroskey, 1998; Dwyer & Davidson, 2012

[2] Speech Communication Association, 1973, December

[3] Ibid

[4] Dwyer & Davidson, 2012

CHAPTER TWO
Definitions and Assessments

    "Speech anxiety" is one term, among many, that people use to describe their nervousness, uneasiness, or even fear of public speaking. "Communication apprehension" (CA) is the scholarly term used by communication researchers to describe a fear or anxiety about communication. There are four different types of CA and each can be self-assessed by level.[1] The following chapter will help you understand the definitions and types of CA, and help you assess your CA levels and communication goals.

2.1 The Academic Definition: Communication Apprehension

Communication apprehension (CA) is defined as "the fear or anxiety associated with real or anticipated communication with others."2 Although "fear," "uneasiness," or "nervousness" about public speaking are words you may use interchangeably with the term speech anxiety, communication apprehension (abbreviated CA) is the academic or scholarly term for speech anxiety. It is the search term you would use most often when looking for articles on CA in communication research and journals.

CA is an emotional response that an individual can have toward communication. If you answer "yes" to either or both of these questions, you have experienced CA in a public speaking context:

1. Have you ever experienced fear, anxiety, or nervousness while simply *anticipating* you will be speaking in front of others? Yes No

2. Have you ever experienced fear, anxiety, or nervousness while delivering a speech or speaking in front of others? Yes No

Sally (banking-mortgage analyst), age 40, said: "I used to nervously anticipate giving a speech. The moment I heard I had to give a speech, I could feel the nervousness in my body. My stomach would start feeling sick about a week before the speech. I would not be able to sleep for at least two nights before the speech. On the day of my presentation, my entire body would start trembling and my stomach would be in knots. The moment I started to speak I could feel my face turn bright red and I would experience intense nervousness… I was so glad to hear that there's help for people like me. Communication anxiety can be conquered."

2.2 Four Types of Communication Apprehension

Communication research identifies at least four types of CA: (1) traitlike, (2) generalized-context, (3) person group, and (4) situational.[3]

Traitlike CA is defined as a "relatively enduring personality-type orientation toward a given mode of communication across a wide variety of contexts."[4] In other words, if you have traitlike CA, you experience anxiety in many circumstances where you might have to communicate with others--in one-on-one conversations, in interviews, in small groups, in discussions with others, in public, and in almost every situation except with family members or a few close friends. About 20 percent of our population experience traitlike CA. [5]

Generalized-Context CA (abbreviated Context CA) is a consistently anxious response and orientation toward communication in a specific setting or context. This means every time you are in a particular context (e.g., public speaking) you experience communication anxiety. There are four common contexts where CA occurs: (1) public speaking, (2) meetings, (3) group discussions, and (4) interpersonal conversations. The most common form of context CA is anxiety related to public speaking. If you experience context CA, you may feel anxiety in a particular context but not in others. For example, you could experience anxiety about speaking in front of others, but not in interpersonal conversations or small group discussions.

Person-Group CA (also called Audience CA) is defined as "a relatively enduring orientation toward communication with a given person or group of people." People who experience audience CA will feel anxiety when communicating with a given person or group of people. For example, you might experience audience CA whenever you talk with someone of higher status at work such as a manager or supervisor, or in an educational experience such as a college professor, or even with someone who is particularly abrupt such as colleague or acquaintance. Most people feel apprehensive when communicating with at least some individuals, so audience CA is quite common.[6]

Situational CA is an emotional response of an individual to communicating with another person or persons at a given time. [7] It is usually short-lived or fleeting; when the situation passes, the anxiety goes away. Most people have experienced situational CA— at least sometime in their lives. For example, you may have felt situational CA during an important job interview, or while taking an oral exam. When the interview or exam was over, your anxiety disappeared.

Because speech anxiety is context CA, this book specifically addresses CA in the public speaking context. The techniques presented here are designed to help you conquer public speaking anxiety, fear, and nervousness that can easily inhibit your career, educational, or social goals. Although you could also use these techniques to help you manage communication anxiety in meetings, group discussions, and interpersonal conversations contexts, the focus here is speaking in front of others.

2.3 Assessment of Communication Apprehension

So far you have learned that CA is based on your emotions and feelings associated with communication. Most people experience at least situational CA or audience CA at various times when the communication is important or the persons involved are of higher status than the speaker. However, some may also experience traitlike CA (across many situations, audiences, and times) or context CA (related to a particular setting). Although you could probably identify the contexts for your CA from the descriptions in the last section, it will be helpful for you to determine your level of CA for each context, so you can monitor your progress over the next few weeks.

Dr. James McCroskey developed the "Personal Report of Communication Apprehension" (PRCA- 24) — a survey to help individuals self-assess their CA levels in the four contexts. After tabulating your answers, you will find the survey produces five scores, including an overall score as well as four context sub scores, including group discussions, meetings, interpersonal conversations, and public speaking. [8] Please complete the survey in Exercise 2.3 and then follow the directions for tabulating each of your sub scores to assess your CA levels.

Exercise 2.3 Personal Report of Communication Apprehension (PRCA-24) Survey[9]

Name   **Date**

Directions: This instrument is composed of twenty-four statements concerning feelings about communicating with other people. Please indicate in the space provided at the end of each question the degree to which each statement applies to you by marking whether you

(1) Strongly agree, (2) agree, (3) are undecided, (4) disagree, (5) strongly disagree.

1. ____I dislike participating in group discussions.
2. ____Generally, I am comfortable while participating in group discussions.
3. ____I am tense and nervous while participating in group discussions.
4. ____I like to get involved in group discussions.
5. ____Engaging in a group discussion with new people makes me tense and nervous.
6. ____I am calm and relaxed while participating in group discussions.
7. ____Generally, I am nervous when I have to participate in a meeting.
8. ____Usually I am calm and relaxed while participating in a meeting.
9. ____I am very calm and relaxed when I am called upon to express an opinion at a meeting.

10. ____I am afraid to express myself at meetings.
11. ____Communicating at meetings usually makes me uncomfortable.
12. ____I am very relaxed when answering questions at a meeting.
13. ____While participating in a conversation with a new acquaintance, I feel very nervous.
14. ____I have no fear of speaking up in conversations.
15. ____Ordinarily I am very tense and nervous in conversations.
16. ____Ordinarily I am very calm and relaxed in conversations.
17. ____While conversing with a new acquaintance, I feel very relaxed.
18. ____I'm afraid to speak up in conversations.
19. ____I have no fear of giving a speech.
20. ____Certain parts of my body feel very tense and rigid while I am giving a speech.
21. ____I feel relaxed while giving a speech.
22. ____My thoughts become confused and jumbled when I am giving a speech.
23. ____I face the prospect of giving a speech with confidence.

24. ___While giving a speech, I get so nervous I forget facts I really know.

Transfer Your PRCA-24 Survey Scores

To tabulate your scores, you will need to first transfer your survey scores from the previous page to the chart on the following page. So please tear out the previous page with your survey answers and place it next to the Tabulating Your Scores chart on the next page to make the transfer and tabulation process easy.

You will use the Norms Chart below after you have transferred and tabulated your scores. Please refer to this page after you have tabulated your scores.

Norms Chart

To interpret your scores, you can compare your scores with the thousands of people who have also completed the PRCA-24. See the following "Norms Chart for the PRCA-24."

Norms Chart for the PRCA-24[16]

Context	Average Score	Average Range	High CA Scores
Group	15.4	11 to 20	21 & Above
Meeting	16.4	12 to 21	22 & Above
Conversation	14.5	10 to 18	19 & Above
Pub Speak	19.3	14 to 24	25 & Above
Overall	65.6	50 to 80	81 & Above

Tabulating Your Scores

Name   **Date**

SCORING: To tabulate your scores, please write your scores from the PRCA-24 survey in the corresponding cells below (next to the appropriate item number in parenthesis). Next add or subtract for each item across each row as indicated. Please note that "18" is a constant so all your sub-scores will be computed by starting with a number of "18 and adding and subtracting as indicated."

Context	ADD scores to 18 for item numbers					MINUS scores for item numbers				Context Scores
Group	18	+(2)__	+(4)__	+(6)__	=__	-(1)__	-(3)__	-(5)__	=____
Meetings	18	+(2)__	+(4)__	+(6)__	=__	-(1)__	-(3)__	-(5)__	=____
Conver-sations	18	+(2)__	+(4)__	+(6)__	=__	-(1)__	-(3)__	-(5)__	=____
Public Speaking	18	+(2)__	+(4)__	+(6)__	=__	-(1)__	-(3)__	-(5)__	=____
Overall	**Add all Four Context Subscores for an overall score=>**								

Your Scores Chart (Write your scores in the chart below . Compare them to the Norms Chart on the previous page. Check (√) your anxiety level based on the Norms.)

CONTEXT & OVERALL	YOUR SCORES	CHECK (√) YOUR LEVEL		
		Low	Average	High
Group				
Meetings				
Conversations				
Public Speaking				
Overall				

As you can read in the chart, your overall score can range from 24 to 120. The average overall score is 65.6, and the average range of scores is 50 to 80. If your overall score is near 65, then it is about normal. If it falls between 50 and 80, it may be a bit above average or below average but it is still within the normal range. If your overall score is above 80, you can conclude that you have a higher than average level of CA. If your overall score is below 50, then you can conclude that you have a lower than average level of CA.

Scores for each of the four contexts—group discussions, meetings, interpersonal conversations, and public speaking--can range from 6 to 30. Any subscore above 18 indicate you have some degree of communication apprehension in a specific context. Notice that the average public speaking score is above 18, which indicates most people tend to be apprehensive about public speaking. Now return to "Your PRCA Scores Chart" and check (√) the level for each of your scores in comparison to the

The Norms chart will give you a good assessment of your overall CA level as well as your CA level in the four contexts. You will easily see if you need the help from this book to learn the techniques to conquer you CA? **If so, keep reading. There is help for you!**

2.4 Research in Communication Apprehension

Did you know that many bright and talented people report they once experienced anxiety and nervousness about speaking or performing in public, including, Winston Churchill, John Fitzgerald Kennedy, Margaret Thatcher, Barbara Walters, Johnny Carson, and Barbra Streisand?[10] These and many others have reported that their anxiety about public speaking once made them feel stupid, less intelligent than others, weak and even cowardly. The communication research shows anxiety about public speaking has nothing to do with a person's intelligence or talents or gender. Both men and women experience anxiety about public speaking.

> **Kim (paralegal), age 31**, said: "I used to think that fearing to give a speech meant I was stupid or there was something wrong with me… My husband and my sisters like to speak in front of others so I thought I must not be smart enough to do that… Now I understand that even some of the brightest and most talented people in the world have experienced anxiety about giving a speech and have conquered their nervousness."

Experiencing anxiety or nervousness about giving a speech does not mean you are weak or cowardly or neurotic. Again, communication research reveals that anxiety about public speaking is not related to other kinds of nervous problems. However, the fear or anxiety about public speaking is related to communication avoidance. In other words, the more public speaking anxiety you have, the more you will try to avoid public speaking opportunities or situations. Because we live at a time when communication is highly valued and a part of everything we do, it is very difficult to escape public communication. If you try to avoid it, you will likely lose many opportunities to share your ideas with others and often, those opportunities include important steps that help you reach future goals. For example, a final grade could depend on an oral presentation of a project. A final job interview could include presenting your experience before a panel of executives. Once on the job, a coveted promotion and salary increase could be tied to a position that includes speaking regularly to employee or to community organizations. Avoiding public speaking in any of these situations could lead to losing the good grade you deserve, the job you really wanted, or the career promotion you were hoping to attain.

Public speaking opportunities also present themselves in your social or community life. For example, as best man or maid of honor for a wedding, you could be asked to toast the bride or groom at the wedding reception. Avoiding that opportunity would leave a friend without the love and respect you really wanted or needed to show. Speaking before a school board on behalf of a program needed by your child, speaking as a representative of a cause for an organization you really believe in, or speaking up for a political issue or a candidate you support are all worthy public speaking opportunities that you need to seize instead of avoid.

Fear or anxiety about giving a speech is not abnormal. It is a problem that many have experienced and conquered. You, too, can conquer your anxiety! Deciding to learn and practice the techniques to overcome speech anxiety is one of the best decisions you will ever make. It means that you are moving in a new and right direction to reach your professional, social, and academic goals.

Exercise 2.4: Evaluating Your Goals

Name   **Date**

Because we all tend to avoid what causes fear or anxiety, your speech anxiety may have already caused you to avoid situations and opportunities related to important future goals. Now is a good time to evaluate your future goals, as well as how anxiety about public speaking has affected past goal attainment. Please circle yes or no and write out answers to the following questions:

1. Have you ever avoided a course because it involved public speaking? Yes No   If yes, please explain.

2. Have you ever received a lower grade than you could have earned because you did not participate in class discussions or give an oral report?   Yes No   If yes, please explain.

3. Have you ever avoided taking a job or leadership position because it involved public speaking?   Yes No   If yes, please explain.

4. Has anxiety about public speaking ever kept you from achieving your goals? Yes No   If yes, please explain.

Be encouraged. You no longer have to miss or redirect your goals because of anxiety about public speaking. Speech anxiety can be conquered.

(TEAR-OUT PAGE FOR PRACTICE AND STUDY)

Journaling #2 Activity: Communication Anxiety & Impact

Name   **Date**

Today, write in your journal how communication anxiety has impacted your life. Pondering CA's effects on your life--as well as your future goals--can inspire you to learn the important interventions needed to stop CA's negative impact on your life.

1. Please evaluate and explain how communication anxiety has negatively impacted your life in the following situations

    a. School or academic life

    b. Career or job

    c. Social life or friendships

2. Describe your academic, professional, and social goals that developing public speaking skills will help you attain.

    a. School or academic life

    b. Career or job

    c. Social life or friendships

2. Describe how you would envision your life if you had no fear, anxiety, or nervousness about public speaking.

Chapter Summary

In academic research, speech anxiety is called communication apprehension (CA) in the public speaking context. There are four types of CA: traitlike, generalized-context (or Context CA), person-group (or Audience CA), and situational. The four most common contexts for CA include: public speaking, meetings, group discussions, and interpersonal conversations. The communication research shows that CA is not related to intelligence, gender, or neuroticism. However, research does indicate that people who experience CA do try to avoid public communication. Avoiding communication can impact your career, grades, and social life. Deciding to learn and practice the techniques to overcome your nervousness and anxiety about public speaking means you are moving in the right direction to attain your academic, professional, and social goals.

Review Questions

After reading this chapter, you should be able to answer the following:

1. What is the common academic term and definition for speech anxiety?

2. Define the four types of communication apprehension (CA).

3. Describe the four contexts where CA can occur.

4. Explain the difference between traitlike CA and public speaking CA.

5. What is the most prevalent form of generalized-context CA?

6. List three human characteristics that are not associated with CA.

7. Explain why and how CA can impact a person's academic, professional, and social life.

8. What have you learned about yourself by completing the PRCA-24 and examining your experiences and goals?

9. What might you share with a person who told you they avoid public presentations either on the job or in a group discussion?

10. Who do you identify with most in this chapter--Sally or Kim? Why?

Notes

[1] McCroskey, 1977, p. 78

[2] Levine & McCroskey, 1990

[3] McCroskey, 1997

[4] McCroskey, 1997, p. 85

[5] Richmond & McCroskey, 1998

[6] Richmond & McCroskey, 1998

[7] McCroskey, 1997

[8] Richmond & McCroskey, 1998

[9] Reprinted by permission of the author, Dr. James C. McCroskey, 1998

[10] Ayers, 1994; Manchester, 1967; Seligmann & Peyser, 1994

CHAPTER THREE
Causes of Speech Anxiety

Do you know what causes your public speaking anxiety? Communication researchers have discovered a variety of reasons, and for many, understanding the cause is helpful. Fortunately, even if you never know the reasons for some of your public speaking anxiety, the major techniques for overcoming speech anxiety work regardless of what caused your anxiety. For the purpose of understanding speech anxiety, this chapter will explain six possible causes for anxiety and nervousness about public speaking. They include: (1) learned responses, (2) worrisome thoughts, (3) performance orientation, (4) perceived lack of public speaking skills, (5) excessive activation in body chemistry and (6) situational aspects of the event or the audience.

3.1 Learned Responses

There two underlying causes for traitlike communication anxiety (CA) that could apply to the public speaking context. These learned responses are called reinforcement and modeling.[1]

Reinforcement Theory points out that learned expectations cause behavior.[2] If children receive positive reinforcement for speaking (e.g., praise, pats on the head, smiles, other rewards), they learn to associate positive consequences with communication. They learn to feel confident when speaking with others. On the other hand, if children are punished or given negative reinforcement when they speak at home or school, they quickly learn to associate speaking with negative consequences. In order to avoid the aversive consequences, they avoid communication. Consequently, they develop negative expectations and a traitlike (overall) anxiety about communication. In addition, some children develop a learned helplessness from a random pattern of responses (some negative, some positive) to their communication.[3] Eventually, they to learn to avoid speaking in many situations.

Reinforcement theory also applies to speech anxiety. If, even as a child, you received negative reinforcement in the form of laughter, negative evaluation, or punishment as a result of speaking in front of others, you could have learned an anxiety response to public speaking. From this negative reinforcement, you soon developed expectations of negative consequences for speaking in public. Today, you may still be experiencing that same anxiety response. You may be reacting to those negative expectations of embarrassment or failure that you learned as a child or teenager.

> **Jerry (telemarketing), age 26,** wrote: "When I was in junior high, we had to give a five-minute speech for an English class. I was really scared because I had never given a speech. I spoke for only two minutes and left out half of what I planned to say. The teacher pointed out what a terrible job I did in front of everyone. The other students looked embarrassed for me. Until now, I tried to avoid public speaking because it would only mean more embarrassment and criticism for me. Now I want to change careers so I am glad to hear I can develop a calm response to public speaking."

Modeling (or watching the reactions of others) can also explain a learned anxiety response to communication.[4] Children learn behaviors by watching others as their models. If children see their parents constantly interacting and talking, they learn to interact and talk freely. However, the opposite also is true. If significant others in children's lives model worrisome or even anxious behaviors in regard to communication, children can learn to react in that way too.

You may have learned to be anxious about public speaking by watching the reactions of others. If others whom you admired exhibited a fear or nervousness about public speaking or if you perceived a negative evaluation for those modeling public speaking, you may have learned to have a nervousness and anxiety about public speaking yourself.

THE GOOD NEWS is that even if your speech anxiety is a learned response to past situations, events, or environments, you can learn techniques to alleviate your anxiety. In other words, even if you have learned an anxious response to public speaking, you will be able to learn a new calming response.

3.2 Worrisome Thoughts

Worrisome thoughts (or cognitions) are another cause or driving force behind speech anxiety. According to Desberg and Marsh,[5] the number one cause of stage fright is anxious thoughts of negative evaluation and failure. Other researchers point out that speech anxiety commonly arises when students think they cannot meet the expectations of their audience.[6] But when they learn that their audience is less difficult to please than first expected, their anxieties subside.

> **Lyle (soil conservation technician), age 39, said**: "In regard to public speaking, I always thought everyone was evaluating everything I did and every word I said. I thought no one would like what I have to say. At the very least, I would sound like an idiot or everyone would become bored. I saw the audience as a beast that I could not please. Since I knew I could never be a perfect speaker, I became even more terrified of public speaking. . . . I was glad to learn that most of those thoughts are not true."

Anxiety about negative evaluation and failure is rooted in your thought processes. If you think or mentally predict that you cannot live up to an audience's grand expectations, you will jump to all kinds of conclusions about the audience, the situation, and yourself. An irrational fear (not based on the possibility of physical harm) will grip your mind and nervous system. When you feel the nervous energy, you will use it to confirm your suspicions that the situation is fearful and to be avoided.[7] Your mind will continue to jump to all kinds of negative conclusions and distortions about how bad public speaking really is, how beastly the audience is, and what a fool you will be if you attempt a speech. The fear of becoming anxious will escalate and result in even more fear, anxiety, nervousness, and avoidance of public speaking.

THE GOOD NEWS is that even if your speech anxiety is based in worrisome thoughts of negative evaluation and failure that escalate into even more fear (to the point of being fearful and anxious about the fear), you can change your worrisome thoughts into positive coping statements with techniques for alleviating speech anxiety. In other words, even if you have developed a worrisome, anxious thinking pattern about public speaking, you will be able to learn new truthful, coping, calming, confidence-building thoughts.

3.3 Performance Orientation

Another explanation for the cause of speech anxiety is called a "performance orientation" or "performance perspective."[8] The performance orientation is related to worrisome thoughts of negative evaluation because it also involves erroneous ideas about public speaking.

In the performance orientation, a speaker views public speaking as a situation demanding a perfect, aesthetic impression, elevated language, flawless oratorical skills or eloquence, and a formal, polished, brilliant delivery.[9] The performance orientation views the audience in a hypercritical evaluation mode that makes one small mistake unforgivable. These misconceptions about the formality and demands of public speaking increase worrisome and anxious thoughts, which, in turn, increase anxiety and fear.

> **Michelle (student), age 18,** wrote: "I used to think that public speaking meant I had to speak in a brilliant, flawless way. I knew everyone could give a better speech than me. I felt that if I said one wrong word or sounded boring, I would be an embarrassment. I was glad to learn that public speaking doesn't mean I have to perform eloquently or perfectly. I can be myself."

Even if your speech anxiety is based on a performance perspective that demands formality and perfection to please a hypercritical audience, you can develop a communication orientation to public speaking. This method, based on cognitive-orientation modification or COM Therapy, views public speaking as a communication encounter that relies on the ordinary skills that you use in everyday conversation.[10] The focus is on helping the audience understand your message, not on audience scrutiny of every detail. You can be yourself and speak with ease as you would with friends and family members.

THE GOOD NEWS is that techniques for alleviating speech anxiety will help you change a performance orientation into a communication orientation. A communication orientation will help you shift your thinking about public speaking from a formal speaker-centered performance to an audience-centered and message-focused communication encounter that in turn will help alleviate your anxiety and nervousness.

3.4 Perceived Lack of Public Speaking Skills

Another source of public speaking anxiety is real or perceived lack of skills.[11] Many people feel anxious when they do not know how to behave in a situation. Likewise, in a public speaking context, when speakers do not know what to do or say, anxiety can increase.

> **Chan (surgical technologist), age 22,** said: "I didn't know how to write a speech, let alone give one. Since English isn't my native language, not knowing what to say or do made my nervousness worse. . . . After I learned public speaking skills and what the speechmaking process was all about, I began to feel more confident."

THE GOOD NEWS is that if a lack of public speaking skills causes your speech anxiety, you can learn and develop those skills. Effective public speaking skills are taught in all public speaking fundamentals courses, business and professional speaking workshops, and in organizations devoted to presentational speaking. Because this book is designed as an auxiliary resource for a communication course, you are probably enrolled in a class or workshop where you can learn and develop your skills through practice.

If you are not enrolled in a public speaking or communication course, then once you have practiced the techniques in this book, you should try to enroll in a class where you can learn and practice effective public speaking skills.

3.5 Excessive Activation or Body Chemistry

Anxiety about communication has also been related to a person's excessive activation (physical nervousness) level or body chemistry. Research studies, especially involving children, have found that some children are more easily activated or stressed than others during daily routine activities.[12] Consequently, children with a low tolerance for uncertainty and stress can become easily aroused in stressful circumstances and produce stress related chemicals in their bodies. They would tend to avoid communication and socialization in order to stay calm and evade feeling nervous or stressed.

As an adult, you may experience excessive physical reactions when it comes to public communication. This is not unusual as you may be one who has a high reactivity or anxious arousal index and thus, your physiological reactivity contributes to feelings of anxiety or even panic.[13]   Excessive physiological activation often makes a person feel out of control because it involves trembling hands and feet, dry mouth, nausea, blushing, tense muscles, pounding or rapid heartbeat, temporary memory loss, wavering voice, shortness of breath, nervous gesturing, or swallowing difficulty.[14]   Although physiological arousal is the source of the problem, it is exacerbated when you interpret or label this excessive activation as "bad" and thus try to avoid public speaking and the "bad" activation responses whenever possible. Labeling public speaking and activation as "bad" actually increases public speaking anxiety.

THE GOOD NEWS is that even if your speech anxiety is related to excessive physiological activation, body chemistry, and/or a desire to avoid those "bad" feelings, you can learn to alleviate those responses. You can learn to reduce your physiological sensations so that giving a speech no longer arouses excessive nervousness or an overwhelmingly anxious response. You can learn a new calming response to public speaking, and then you will be able to label a little activation as "normal" or "energizing."

3.6 Situational Aspects

Many aspects of a situation contribute to the amount of speech anxiety a person experiences. These situational causes of speech anxiety include novelty, conspicuousness, and audience characteristics.[15]

Novelty involves a situation that is unfamiliar, an audience that is unfamiliar, or a role that is unfamiliar. If you are speaking in an unfamiliar environment, if you do not know the audience you will be addressing, or if you have seldom given a speech, you may experience a fear of the unknown and an anxiety about how to act. The reverse is also true. The more you participate as a public speaker, the more acclimated you will become to that role and the more you will feel at ease with any audience or situation. Your anxiety from novelty will diminish.

Conspicuousness means attention is focused on something or someone. In the public speaking situation, it is the speaker who stands out from an audience. Although being at the center of attention at first might seem frightening, it also means that your ideas are being heard by others and not ignored. Being conspicuous is part of public speaking, but you can learn to enjoy being the center of attention and knowing that the audience is listening to your ideas. If you are experiencing increased speech anxiety because you are the center of attention, you can learn to see the situation as if you were speaking conversationally to a few friends who are attentively listening to your suggestions.

Audience characteristics such as size, status, similarity, and formality also can contribute to a speaker's anxiety. The larger the number of people in an audience, the higher the status of the people in an audience, and the more dissimilar an audience is in age, gender, education, or culture, the more anxiety some speakers feel. Because formality often requires certain behaviors that allow for little deviation, the more formal a situation seems, the more anxiety the speaker might feel. As with novelty and conspicuousness, the more you participate in public speaking and learn public speaking skills, the more comfortable you will feel in front of any audience regardless of the formality, size, or audience constituents.

Again, there is GOOD NEWS. Even if your speech anxiety is increased with novelty, conspicuousness, or audience characteristics, applying the techniques in this book will help alleviate your speech anxiety. You will learn to manage your anxiety when speaking to a large number of people, a high-status audience, a dissimilar audience, or an audience in formal situations.

Exercise 3.6: Assessing the Causes of Your Speech Anxiety

Name   **Date**

Because it is helpful to understand your speech anxiety before you learn to manage it, now is a good time to assess the sources of your anxiety. Sometimes speech anxiety develops at an age when you cannot recall what instigated it. On the other hand, often you can attribute your anxiety to specific instances. Please write out answers to the following questions in an effort to identify the sources of your anxiety about public speaking.

1. Learned Responses.

a. Can you think of a situation where you learned that speaking in public has negative consequences? Yes No Explain where and when?

b. Can you think of people who may have modeled avoidance or a nervousness of public speaking that you learned to imitate? Yes No

c. If yes, what was each person's relationship to you and what did they model for you?

2. Worrisome Thoughts.

a. Do you have worrisome thoughts about public speaking that include a fear of failure and negative evaluation by the audience? Yes No

b. If yes, describe them.

(TEAR-OUT PAGE FOR PRACTICE AND STUDY)

3. Performance Orientation.

a. Do you view public speaking from a performance orientation where you think you have to use flawless, elevated, and dignified language or a formal, polished, brilliant delivery to be an effective speaker? Yes   No

b. Would you feel less anxious about public speaking if you viewed it from a communication orientation that relies on your everyday conversational skills?   Yes   No

4. Perceived Lack of Skills.

a. Do you believe you lack the skills to be an effective public speaker? Yes   No   Explain your answer.

b. Are you willing to enroll in a class or workshop, learn, and practice the skills needed to become an effective public speaker?   Yes   No

5. Excessive Activation.

a. Do you label public speaking as "bad" because you experience those feelings of excessive activation? Yes   No   Explain your answer.

b. Are you willing to learn techniques to help you feel calm and energized when speaking in public?   Yes   No

6. Situational Aspects.

a. Have you ever experienced communication anxiety because of situational characteristics (novelty, conspicuousness, and audience characteristics)?   Yes   No

b. Describe the situation.

(TEAR-OUT PAGE FOR PRACTICE AND STUDY)

Journaling #3 Activity: What Caused My Speech Anxiety?

Name   **Date**

It is helpful to understand your speech anxiety before you try to conquer it. Consider the six causes listed below.

1. Describe the situations related to any of the six causes that you think contributed to your speech anxiety.

2. Point out which ones you think impacted you the most.

3. Which ones you would like to change the most? Explain your answers.

   a. Learned Responses (situations where you learned that speaking in public has negative consequences or relationships where others modeled avoidance or nervousness about public speaking).

   b. Worrisome Thoughts (public speaking situations where you felt nervous because you feared negative evaluation by the listeners)

   c. Performance Orientation (situations where you felt nervous because you thought public speaking required flawless, dignified language and perfect delivery)

*(*TEAR-OUT PAGE FOR PRACTICE AND STUDY)

d. Perceived Lack of Skills (situations where you wished you had public speaking skills)

e. Excessive Activation (public speaking situations where you experienced excessive activation)

f. Situational Aspects (situations where you felt conspicuous or fearful because all eyes were on you. or because the situation was new. or because the audience was of higher status than you)

(TEAR-OUT PAGE FOR PRACTICE AND STUDY)

Chapter Summary

Researchers have discovered a variety of causes for a person's nervousness of public speaking. These causes include: (1) learned responses, (2) worrisome thoughts, (3) a performance orientation, (4) perceived lack of skills, (5) excessive activation, and (6) situational aspects of the circumstance or audience. However, THERE IS GOOD NEWS FOR EVERYONE. Although people often want to understand what caused their speech anxiety, it is NOT vital to discover the cause in order to find an effective treatment. The techniques presented in this book will help you overcome the anxiety of public speaking. They are supported by substantial communication research and have helped thousands of people reduce their fear, nervousness, and anxiety about public speaking regardless of the causes.

Review Questions

After reading this chapter, you should be able to answer the following:

1. Why is it helpful but not essential to understand the causes of your anxiety about public speaking?

2. What are six possible causes for speech anxiety?

3. Describe an example of a learned response cause of speech anxiety.

4. Explain the differences between reinforcement and modeling.

5. Identify common worrisome thoughts that increase speech anxiety.

6. If, you think you cannot meet your audience's expectations and then you feel nervous energy in your body, what is likely to happen next?

7. Compare and contrast the following views of public speaking: the performance orientation and the communication orientation.

8. How can someone alleviate speech anxiety caused from a perceived lack of public speaking skills?

9. What are some of the physiological symptoms of activation?

10. Explain the three situational causes of speech anxiety.

Notes

[1]Ayres, 1988; Daly, Caughlin, & Stafford, 2009; McCroskey, 1982, Van Kleeck & Daly, 1982)

[2]Daly, Caughlin, & Stafford, 2009; McCroskey, 1982

[3]McCroskey, 1982

[4]Bandura, 1973

[5]Desberg and Marsh, 1988[6]Ayres, 1986

[7]Behnke & Beatty, 1981; Desberg and Marsh, 1988

[8]Motley, 1991, p.88

[9]Motley 1991, 1998

[10]Motley, 1991, 2009

[11]Richmond & McCroskey, 1998

[12]Kagan & Reznick, 1986; Kagan, Reznick, & Snidman, 1988; McCullough, Russell, Behnke, Sawyer, & Witt, 2006

[13]Finn, Sawyer, Behnke, 2009

[14]Gilkerson, 1942; Clevenger & King, 1961; Mulac & Sherman, 1974; Mulac, Wiemann, Moloney, & Marlow, 2009; Pucel & Stocker, 1983; Richmond & McCroskey, 1998

[15]Daly, Caughlin, & Stafford, 2009

CHAPTER FOUR
Excessive Activation and
The Fight-Flight-Freeze Response

Where does all your excessive activation (physical nervousness) come from, or how can your body chemistry be a source of speech anxiety? The "fight-flight-freeze response" is one explanation. When you perceive that a situation is threatening, your brain will stimulate your nervous system to prepare your body for the impending danger. Your body will produce a series of biochemical reactions to energize you. This response was first described by Dr. Walter Cannon of Harvard Medical School as the "fight or flight response." Psychologists have more recently added the "freeze" element to the name because often our bodies become overwhelmed and immobilized from the excessive energy and simply freeze.

4.1 A Perceived Threat

The fight or flight response is an innate involuntary response that was especially important for our primitive ancestors. This instinct protected them from danger. When our early ancestors, who lived in caves and a perilous environment, perceived danger, their bodies produced large bursts of energy to fight off or flee from predators or other environmental hazards. Today, thousands of years later, when we perceive a danger or frightening circumstance, our bodies still produce all the physical energy to flee or fight. If the energy is not expended, the result is excessive activation or freezing immobilization.

The "Fight-Flight-Freeze Response" is defined as an innate biochemical response in our bodies. When our minds perceive a real or imagined threat, the brain is triggered to stimulate the sympathetic nervous system to prepare the body to fight or flee from the situation. The resulting physiological activation and sensations from the biochemical reactions in our bodies are often labeled excessive "nervousness." The resulting behaviors can include: avoiding the situation (fleeing), struggling through the nerve-wracking experience (fighting), or mind-blanking, immobilization (freezing).

4.2 Triggering Nervous Sensations

The fight-flight-freeze response is elicited when we perceive a real or imagined threat. It doesn't matter whether the threat is a real beast or the imagined threat of a beastly audience listening to your speech. The fight- flight-freeze response can be triggered in response to a big animal chasing us or a scary thought or feeling. The perception of a problem, real or imagined, triggers the hypothalamus (master stress-response switch in the brain) to stimulate the sympathetic nervous system (part of the autonomic nervous system) and the endocrine system to release emergency hormones to prepare the body to confront the physical danger. Some of the resulting physiological responses include:

1. Increased heart rate or heart pounding
2. Increased blood pressure
3. Increased perspiration (sweating)
4. Increased breathing or shortness of breath
5. Increased blood sugar for more energy
6. Increased blood flow to the muscles for running or fighting (blood flows away from the hands and feet causing them to feel cold)
7. Locked diaphragm
8. Shut-down of digestion (resulting in stomach upset or nausea)
9. Dry mouth (from increased adrenalin secretion stopping the flow of saliva)
10. Dizziness or lightheadedness
11. Blushing or red-blotchy skin
12. Trembling arms, hands, or feet

All of these sensations are your body's response to prepare you to FIGHT or FLEE and can result in a FREEZING reaction. The freezing reaction is much like stepping on the accelerator (arousal) and brakes (immobilization) in your car, at the same time causing the mind to become paralyzed in thinking. [3]

4.3 Halting the Fight-Flight-Freeze Response

If you perceive public speaking as threatening, your brain signals your sympathetic nervous system to prepare your body to confront or flee the danger. Physically, you are prepared to fight a wild beast or flee for your life-- much more physical preparation than you need for giving a speech. Hence, you feel all the excessive nervous energy that can immobilize you or stymie your presentation: a pounding or racing heartbeat, shortness of breath, increased perspiration, dry mouth, nausea, indigestion, cold hands and feet, trembling hands and feet, wavering voice, blushing face, fidgeting, dizziness, or tingling sensations.[4]

In order to counter or turn off the excessive activation and physical sensations of nervousness, you must stop the fight-flight-freeze response from activating. You can halt this response by (1) stopping the worrisome thoughts that alert your brain to a threat or (2) bringing on a relaxation response – quieting the sympathetic nervous system and helping the parasympathetic nervous system to bring equilibrium to your body again.[5]

The technique called *cognitive restructuring*, presented in Chapter Seven, will help you stop the worrisome thought patterns that trigger the fight-flight-freeze response. When there is no perception of a threat, the fight-flight-freeze response will not be activated. In addition, systematic desensitization (SD) presented in Chapter Eight, and deep abdominal breathing, presented in Chapter Six, will help you develop a calming relaxation response to public speaking. Because fear and relaxation are incompatible, SD and deep abdominal breathing will help shut down the fight-flight-freeze response. When it is shut down, excessive activation--including the aggravating sensations of a pounding heartbeat, nausea, trembling limbs, wavering voice, flushed face, dry mouth, and increased perspiration--will be minimized or eliminated.

> **Joi (banking management), age 25,** said: "One time I was asked to give a speech. Even though I would get very nervous about public speaking, I said, "yes" because it was part of an important job promotion I wanted. On the day of the speech, I showed up early at the meeting room. As people began to arrive, my heart started racing, my shirt became wet with perspiration, and I felt sick to my stomach. When my boss came over to my chair, I asked to be excused for a drink of water. I couldn't think straight so I walked out of the room, out of the building and out of the job. After I learned about the fight-flight- freeze response and how to apply the anxiety reduction techniques to stop it, I never have to run from a speech again."

Exercise 4.3: Assess Your Activation and Sensations

Name   **Date**

Since the fight-flight-freeze response activates many physiological sensations, it is a good idea to assess what sensations are being activated/

1. Please check (√) the sensations you experience <u>when delivering</u> a speech.

Nervous Sensations		Delivering a Speech (√)	Thinking about an upcoming speech (√)
a.	Pounding or rapid heartbeat		
b.	Blushing or red face		
c.	Perspiring		
d.	Shortness of breath		
e.	Cold hands or feet		
f.	Trembling hands or feet		
g.	Nausea or indigestion		
h.	Dizziness or tingling sensations		
i.	Fidgeting or nervous gesturing		
j.	Wavering voice		
k.	Forgetting your thoughts or place		

2. Please check the sensation listed above that you experience when you <u>anticipate or are thinking</u> about an upcoming public speaking opportunity.

3. How is the fight-flight-freeze response causing your excessive activation, including nervous sensations before, during, and even after you speak.

(TEAR-OUT PAGE FOR PRACTICE AND STUDY)

Journaling #4 Activity: My Fight-Flight-Freeze Response

Name   **Date**

Today in your journal, you will evaluate if and how you are perceiving public speaking as a physical or psychological threat. Use the following points to guide your journaling:

1. What do you think is causing you to perceive public speaking as a threat?

2. Picture in your mind your last public speaking experience (or an especially anxious time when you spoke in front of others). Describe any of the fight-flight-freeze reactions that you experienced and when you started experiencing them (e.g., the night before the speech and one hour before the speech).

3. Describe the situation and how you would feel if you did not have to experience the fight-flight-freeze reactions and physical sensations

4. Which techniques are you looking forward to learning in order to stop your fight-flight-freeze reactions? Why?

(TEAR-OUT PAGE FOR PRACTICE AND STUDY)

Chapter Summary

Excessive activation can be explained by the fight-flight-freeze response. This response is an instinctive and involuntary response brought on by the perception of impending danger. When your brain perceives a threat, it triggers the body to stimulate the nervous system to release chemicals that prepare you to fight or flee the danger. These chemical reactions are responsible for many of your nervous sensations--increased heartbeat, increased perspiration, increased breathing, nausea, dry mouth, trembling limbs, cold hands and feet, wavering voice--and can cause you to freeze and forget your thoughts too. You can halt the fight-flight-freeze response by either stopping the worrisome thoughts that alert your brain to a threat or calling forth a relaxation response to quiet your nervous system. The techniques of cognitive restructuring, systematic desensitization, and diaphragmatic breathing will help inactivate the fight-flight-freeze response. When the fight-flight-freeze response is inactivated, your nervous sensations will be minimized or eliminated.

Review Questions

After reading this chapter, you should be able to answer the following:

1. How is excessive physical activation related to the fight-flight-freeze response?

2. Explain how the fight or flight response was an important and helpful response for our primitive ancestors.

3. Explain why the fight-flight-freeze response is not helpful for public speakers who perceive public speaking as a threatening situation.

4. List the nervous sensations or responses that you experience related to fight-flight-freeze.

5. How can the fight-flight-freeze response be halted?

6. What techniques will you use to stop the fight-flight-freeze response?

Notes

[1]Benson, 1975; Benson & Klippper, 2000; Cannon, 1914; Levine, 1997

[2]Dr. Walter Cannon, 1914; Levine, 1997

[3]Benson, 1975; Davis, Eshelman, & McKay, 2000; Levine, 1997; Smith, Sawyer, Behnke, 2005

[4]Clevenger & King, 1961; Gilkerson, 1942; Pucel & Stocker, 1983; Richmond & McCroskey, 1998; Behnke & Beatty 1981, Behnke, & Sawyer, 1999, 2000, 2001a, 2001b, 2004

[5]Benson, 1975; Jacobson, 1938; Rice, 1987, 1998

Part Two: Treating Speech Anxiety

CHAPTER FIVE
A Multidimensional Plan for
Conquering Speech Anxiety

This chapter will help you choose techniques for developing a personalized program to conquer your speech anxiety. The program relies on a multidimensional and combinational approach to treating speech anxiety. The combinational approach is based on communication research that shows the greatest reduction in public speaking anxiety is achieved when a combination of techniques are used, instead of only a single treatment.[1] The multidimensional approach is based on the multimodal counseling model that emphasizes the importance of matching treatment techniques to each of seven human personality dimensions.[2] Because it is important to use a combination of techniques, this chapter will show you how to match specific techniques to your personality dimensions so you can select the combination that will be most useful to you.

5.1 Assess Your Personality Dimensions Affected By Anxiety

Each of us has seven dimensions that make up our personalities.[3] Since we are "biological beings who move, feel, sense, imagine, think, and relate to one another, each of these dimensions requires our attention when problems emerge." [4] Consequently, treatment for speech anxiety, like any other problem that affects our emotions, can best be addressed from a multidimensional perspective.

The seven interactive personality dimensions that should be considered in any multidimensional evaluation process include behavior, affect, sensation, imagery, cognition, interpersonal relationships, and drugs/biological functions.[5] The acronym **BASICS** is a helpful tool for remembering these dimensions. In this acronym, two of the dimensions, interpersonal relationships and drugs/biological functions, relate to ways to deal with stress in your life and are combined into one new dimension called stress. Here is a description for each of the BASICS personality dimensions:

B=BEHAVIOR (overt behaviors, acts, habits, and reactions that can be observed and measured)

A=AFFECT (emotions, moods, and strong feelings)

S=SENSATION (bodily sensations, such as pain, tension, discomfort, or nausea; and the touching, tasting, smelling, seeing, and hearing of our five senses)

I=IMAGERY (vivid scenes, pictures, or images that come to mind including the way you see yourself in particular situations)

C=COGNITION (thoughts, attitudes, ideas, beliefs, or opinions)

S=STRESS (amount of stress in your life and ways you deal with it; general physical well-being, use of drugs or alcohol, participation in exercise programs, interactions with others and interpersonal support).

The BASICS dimensions can function as an educational guide to help you analyze your anxiety.[7] When the BASICS multidimensional assessment is applied to your anxiety about public speaking, you can determine which technique you should begin using as well as which combination of techniques will be most helpful to you. Consequently, a multidimensional assessment of your BASICS is the first step in creating a personalized plan to conquer your speech anxiety. To assess the personality dimensions involved in your speech anxiety, please complete Exercise 5.1.

Exercise 5.1: Assess Your BASICS Personality Dimensions

Name   Date

Please respond to the statements below in order to assess speech anxiety in each of your personality dimensions. You may notice some or all of these dimensions involved in your speech anxiety:

1. **BEHAVIOR** refers to observable acts, habits, or behaviors. In regard to your speech anxiety, list the behaviors in a public speaking situation you would like to learn, change, decrease, or increase. (For example, I need to learn speech outlining, delivery skills, how to fulfill the time requirement, and how to use fewer "uhms.")

2. **AFFECT** refers to emotions, moods, and strong feelings. In regard to your speech anxiety, list the emotions or strong feelings you experience while preparing or delivering a speech. (For example, I experience overwhelming nervousness, anxiety, and feelings of impending doom.)

3. **SENSATION** refers to physical sensations (i.e., pain, tension, discomfort, nausea) and the feelings of the five senses. In regard to your speech anxiety, list the negative bodily sensations that you experience before, during, or immediately after you give a public presentation. (For example, I feel stomach butterflies, or dry mouth.)

4. **IMAGERY** refers to vivid scenes, pictures, or images that come to mind, including the way you see yourself. In regard to your speech anxiety, describe the negative ways you "picture yourself" and your surroundings when you deliver a speech. (For example, I imagine my entire audience laughing or snickering at me. I see myself overwhelmed with nervousness or passed out on the floor..)

5. **COGNITION** refers to your thoughts, attitudes, ideas, beliefs, or opinions. In regard to your speech anxiety, describe your negative thoughts and condemning self-talk about giving a speech. (For example, I cannot meet the audience's demands--they expect me to give a perfect speech; I know I will make a mistake, sound stupid, and look like a fool.)

6. **STRESS** refers to the amount of stress in your life, your general physical well-being, your use of drugs or alcohol, and your exercise or health programs, as well as the interpersonal support (or lack of it) that you receive from significant others. In regard to your speech anxiety, describe the stress in your life, your stress reduction activities or exercise programs, and any support or lack of support you experience in your interpersonal relationships. (For example, I am always stressed because of work, school, and family. I seldom exercise or get enough sleep. I have no stress reduction plan. My roommate laughs at me when I practice a speech.)

Now that you know which of your personality dimensions are involved in your speech anxiety, you are ready to discover which dimension initiates your speech anxiety by "tracking the firing order."

(TEAR-OUT PAGE FOR PRACTICE AND STUDY)

5.2 Track Your Firing Order: Get to the Root of Your Anxiety

"Tracking the firing order" means pinpointing the personality dimension where your speech anxiety initiates (fires) and the sequence of dimensions that fire in your speech anxiety."[8] Tracking the firing order will help you determine which anxiety-reduction technique to use.

In other words, tracking firing order gets at the root of your speech anxiety. Once you know the root of your speech anxiety, you can choose the techniques most fitted to the place your nervousness begins. Treating speech anxiety at its initiating point in your personality will result in the most permanent change and reduction of anxiety.

Determining the best technique for treating CA does not diminish the importance of learning more than one anxiety-reduction technique. Tracking the firing order can be compared to lining up dominoes or blocks in a "snake formation" as you might have done as a child. When you pushed over the first domino, a chain reaction occurred; the remainder snaked along and toppled over quickly. If you stopped the first domino from falling, the remaining dominoes had a greater chance of staying upright. In the same way, your goal in tracking the firing order is to locate the first domino (dimension where your speech anxiety begins) and then to keep it from falling (stop the speech anxiety from developing there). Next, locate the second domino (the second dimension where your speech anxiety fires) and stop it from setting off the chain reaction. If you can determine where your speech anxiety starts and then treat that dimension with one of the techniques, you can limit the chain reaction and lessen the effects CA has on your personality. See the following two examples.

> **Sarah, (hotel manager) age 31,** said: "When I have to speak at a meeting, I suddenly feel my heart pound and my face turn bright red before it's my turn to get up. Then I think, 'Oh, this is terrible; I've lost control--people will notice how nervous I am.' I picture myself passed out on the floor with everyone staring at me and then fear overwhelms me."

In Sarah's situation, speech anxiety begins in the sensation dimension (i.e., she physically feels her heart pound and her face turn bright red). The firing order or sequence of dimensions involved in Sarah's speech anxiety is (1) sensation (she physically feels), (2) cognition (she thinks), (3) imagery (she imagines), and (4) affect (she emotionally feels). The first technique for Sarah to practice and the one most effective for managing Sarah's speech anxiety will be the one targeted to the source of her problem--the SENSATION DIMENSION.

> **John, (military flight assistant) age 24,** said: "I always think that people at work will laugh at my ideas and I will sound stupid. Then I imagine people staring at me while I say something stupid or stand frozen--forgetting my entire train of thought. Next, I feel my heart pound, my stomach turn, and my mouth get dry. Fear overcomes me."

In John's situation, speech anxiety begins in the cognition dimension. He thinks people will laugh at him and he will sound stupid. The firing order or sequence of dimensions involved in John's speech anxiety is (1) cognition (he thinks), (2) imagery (he imagines), (3) sensation (he physically feels), and (4) affect (he emotionally feels). The first technique for John to practice and the most effective one for managing John's speech anxiety will be the one targeted to the source of his problem--the COGNITION DIMENSION.

Your goal is to find the top dimension in your firing order for speech anxiety so that you can begin by applying a treatment technique to it. In addition, you will want to look for the sequence of dimensions (especially the top three dimensions) involved in your speech anxiety so you can choose techniques that fit those dimensions and thus, form a program or plan tailored to you. In the next exercise, you will track the firing order of dimensions involved in your speech anxiety.

Exercise 5.2: Track Your Firing Order

Name   **Date**

In order to track your firing order, you will need to determine where your speech anxiety begins. Answer these questions to help you decide, which dimension of your personality initiates your fear, anxiety, or nervousness.

1. Imagine your employer or supervisor has just told you that you must give a speech to twenty-five people within the next hour. Next, try to rank order the dimensions that fire in your speech anxiety (1, 2, 3, 4, 5, and 6). Give special attention to ranking the top three dimensions (1, 2, and 3).

    a. Do you immediately think "Having to give a speech will be awful? I can't do it! Everyone will laugh at me or think less of me. I will make a fool of myself." If irrational, negative, or unproductive thoughts are the first to fire, the top of your firing order is COGNITION. _____

    b. Do you immediately feel (physically) any of the following sensations (even before a thought enters your mind) such as nausea or stomach tightness, heart racing, heart palpitations, blushing, sweating, lightheadedness, or other physiological reactions? If bodily sensations are the first to fire, the top of your firing order is SENSATION. _____

    c. Do you immediately and vividly visualize yourself in a scene where you faint in front of the audience, are the focus of audience laughter or jeers, run out of the room, or are engaged in any other negative activity? If negative mental pictures are the first to fire, the top of your firing order is IMAGERY. _____

    d. Do you immediately feel (emotionally) upset, anxious, or nervous? If emotional feelings of nervousness or anxiety are the first to fire, the top of your firing order is AFFECT. _____

    e. Do you immediately react with avoidant behaviors, such as procrastination or running from the situation? Do you avoid public speaking because you have no skills? If avoidant behaviors related to lack of public speaking skills are the first to fire, then the top of your firing order is BEHAVIOR. _____

f.   Do you feel overstressed in general so that giving a speech just adds one more stressful situation to your already stressful lifestyle in which you get very little exercise, are overworked, take drugs or alcohol to cope, eat poorly, or experience little social support? If stress in general, use of drugs, poor physical health, and lack of mutually supportive friendships fires first, the top of your firing order is STRESS. _____

2. Which dimension is at the top of your firing order (ranked #1)?

3. List the firing order of the top three dimensions involved in your speech anxiety (ranked #1, #2, #3).

(TEAR-OUT PAGE FOR PRACTICE AND STUDY)

5.3 Match Treatment to Personality Dimensions

Once you know the firing order of the dimensions involved in your speech anxiety, you can easily decide which technique to begin using. The following techniques with the personality dimension that each target will help you select the technique that matches the top of your firing order:

1. ***Cognitive Restructuring*** targets the cognitive dimension. If cognition is at the top of your firing order, begin using cognitive Restructuring.

2. ***Systematic Desensitization*** targets the affect, sensation, and imagery dimensions. If affect, sensation, or imagery is at the top of your firing order, begin using systematic desensitization.

3. ***Mental Rehearsal*** (visualization) targets the imagery and cognitive dimensions. If imagery or cognition is at the top of your firing order, concentrate on using mental rehearsal.

4. ***Diaphragmatic Breathing*** targets the affect and sensation dimensions. If affect or sensation is at the top of your firing order, begin using deep abdominal breathing (it is an important part of systematic desensitization and mental rehearsal, too).

5. ***Physical Exercise and Stress*** reduction routines target the stress dimension. If stress is at the top of your firing order, contact your physician and work with a professional on developing a stress reduction program for your life and a healthier lifestyle. Also, try to enroll in a workshop or class designed specifically to help individuals overcome speech anxiety, especially one that will provide a supportive environment where you can develop supportive friends working on the same public speaking goals.

6. ***Skills Training*** targets the behavior dimension. If behavior is at the top of your firing order, you should immediately enroll in a public speaking class or seminar where you can learn and practice public speaking skills. (The class should include delivering speeches and helping you set new goals for each speech.)

Personal Notes

Exercise 5.3: Match Techniques to Personality Dimensions

Name   **Date**

Once you have assessed your personality dimensions in Exercise 5.1 and tracked your firing order in Exercise 5.2, you are ready to match techniques to the top three dimensions in your firing order.

1. Using the chart on the previous page and referring to Exercise 5.2, please list the top three dimensions in your firing order. Start with the dimension ranked #1.

My Firing Order of Dimensions--The Top Three

RANK	YOUR DIMENSION	SPEECH ANXIETY– REDUCTION TECHNIQUE
#1		
#2		
#3		

2. Next, refer to the following list of speech anxiety–reduction techniques targeted to each personality dimension and complete your chart with the techniques matched to your top three dimensions.

(TEAR-OUT PAGE FOR PRACTICE AND STUDY)

Basics Personality Dimensions & Anxiety–Reduction Techniques

DIMENSION	SPEECH ANXIETY–REDUCTION TECHNIQUE
Behavior	Skills Training (enroll in a public speaking workshop, class, or club where you can learn and practice public speaking skills)
Affect	Systematic Desensitization & Diaphragmatic Breathing
Sensation	Systematic Desensitization & Diaphragmatic Breathing
Imagery	Systematic Desensitization & Mental Rehearsal (Visualization)
Cognitive	Cognitive Restructuring &/or Mental Rehearsal
Stress & Interpersonal Relationships	Interpersonal Support or Physical Exercise Programs & Stress-Reduction Plans (contact your physician to help you start a stress reduction and physical exercise program or enroll in a class or workshop or club where you can receive support from others who also desire to overcome speech anxiety)

Start with the Technique that Matches the Top of Your Firing Order

Now you know what techniques to begin using. Because your goal is to apply a technique to the top of your firing order in order to get at the root of your speech anxiety, focus on the technique (or techniques, if tied) that matches the dimension ranked #1 in your firing order. Next, apply a technique to the dimension ranked #2 in your firing order and then to the one ranked #3.

This is important: Matching techniques to personality dimensions in your firing order should not become something so precise that you begin to worry if you have truly found the top of your firing order. Tracking the firing order should simply serve as a guide to help you determine which techniques will be most effective for you. Many people report that it helps them understand why one technique works better for one person, while another works better for someone else. The techniques that will work best for you will target the dimensions at the top of your firing order.

Some report that what they thought, at first, was the top of their firing order really turned out to be ranked second or third as they began using the techniques. Others report that it was difficult to choose between two dimensions (which one ranked #1 and which one ranked #2 in their firing order). That, too, is not a problem. Start applying techniques to the top two or three dimensions in your firing order. Remember, a combinational approach (using at least two or more techniques) will work best at helping you overcome speech anxiety. Also keep in mind that your goal in the multidimensional approach is to apply techniques to all of the dimensions involved in your speech anxiety.

When you have applied techniques at every personality dimension involved in your speech anxiety, beginning with the technique that fits the top of your firing order, you will experience a substantial reduction in your fear, nervousness and anxiety about public speaking. You will be on the road to becoming a confident speaker.

5.4 Commit Time to Actively Learning the Techniques

The techniques that you matched to your firing order of dimensions in Exercise 5.3 will be presented in the remainder of this book. However, before you read about them, you need to make a commitment of time to really learn and practice the techniques. Knowing a little bit about them versus having a hands-on working knowledge of them are two different things.

Active learning means more than passively reading about something. Active learning means that you understand what you read and actually write down responses to the exercises. It means that you keep a journal of your progress.

Practicing the techniques means you will work with them until you can apply them at a moment's notice. You will need to follow the directions and suggestions in order to get the most benefit out of the techniques

5.5 Develop a Personal Plan and Practice Schedule

The best way to stay on track with practicing the techniques is to develop a personal plan and practice schedule. This is part of your commitment to overcoming speech anxiety. Determine how much time you can spend practicing the techniques, which ones you need to learn (those that fit your firing order), and then schedule sessions using an engagement calendar, just as you would any other important event. Using Exercise 5.5, develop your personal plan and practice schedule for the next three weeks. Be realistic in scheduling the time you can set aside for practice sessions. Try to set aside thirty to sixty minutes per day to review this book and practice the techniques. The speed of your progress is directly related to the time you spend practicing the techniques.

When planning your practice schedule, try to make the technique that fits the top of your firing order a priority. Then do the same with the second and third techniques based on your firing order of dimensions (refer to Exercises 5.2 and 5.3). Finally, include the remainder of the techniques that relate to your BASICS dimensions. Once you have developed your personal plan and practice schedule, you will be more likely to follow it.

Exercise 5.5: My Three-Week Plan and Practice Schedule

Name   **Date**

Using the chart below, plan your personal practice schedule for the next three weeks.* See Kim's example on the following page to help you further understand this exercise. Be sure to place the technique that fits the top of your firing order on your schedule first. Try to include a few hours weekly to read this book, answer the questions, and keep a journal.

1. My firing order of dimensions includes these three dimensions:

2. The techniques I need to learn and practice include:

*Develop Your Practice Schedule: Date, Techniques, and Times**

Sunday	Monday	Tuesday	Wednesday	Thursday	Friday	Saturday

*When you have finished working with your schedule, record exact times in an engagement calendar. Post this schedule where you can see it daily to remind you of your commitment.

(TEAR-OUT PAGE FOR PRACTICE AND STUDY)

Example: Kim's Schedule, Techniques, & Time Commitment

Key: CR = Cognitive Restructuring; DB = Diaphragmatic Breathing; SD = Systematic Desensitization

Sunday	Monday	Tuesday	Wednesday	Thursday	Friday	Saturday
7pm Read book & Do exercises =60 min	*8am* CR =30 min	*9pm* Read book & Exercises =50 min	*[7 am* Read book & CR =60 min *3pm* DB=5 min	*7 am* MCR=2 min *10 am* DB=5 min	*7am* DB=5 min, & MCR=2 min *9 pm* Read book& SD=60 min	*7am* DB=5 min, MCR=2 min. *4pm* PE=30 min
7am DB=5 min, & MCR=2 min *9 pm* Read book& SD=60 min	*7am* DB=5 min, MCR=2 min, *4pm* PE=30 min	*7am* DB=5 min, & MCR=2 min *9pm* Read book & SD=60 min	*7am* DB=5 min, MCR=2 min	*7am* DB=5 min, & MCR=2 min *9pm* SD=35 min	*7am* DB=5 min, MCR=2 min *10pm* VIS=10 min	*7am* DB=5 min, MCR=2 min *4pm* PE=30 min
7am DB=5 min, MCR=2 min *4pm* PE=30 min	*7am* DB=5 min, & MCR=2 min *9 pm* SD=35 min	*7am* DB=5 min, MCR=2 min *10pm* VIS=10 min	*7am* DB=5 min, & MCR=2 min *9 pm* SD=35 min	*7am* DB=5 min, & MCR=2 min *10pm* VIS=10 min	*7am* DB=5 min, & MCR=2 min *10pm* VIS=10 min	*7am* DB=5 min, & MCR=2 min *10am* PE=30 min

5.6 Keep a Journal of Your Progress

In addition to monitoring your time, please keep a journal of your thoughts and feelings, as well as changes in your communication anxiety level. Journaling has been found to be a therapeutic aid in helping individuals face, tolerate, and manage many physical and psychological stresses. In fact, emotionally expressing and mentally processing stressful events in journal writing has brought many positive benefits to the journal writer.[9] "Writing is considered powerful because when individuals translate experiences into language, they begin a cognitive process of structuring and organizing these experiences into smaller and easier to handle events."[10] As thoughts about events change, significant positive growth is experienced and reported by those who journal.[11]

To get started on journaling, respond to the journaling activity and questions at the end of every chapter. (You should have started doing this in Chapter One.) Record your feelings after each practice session and any opportunity you have to do public speaking (e.g., in class, on the job, at a meeting, etc.). Be sure to record the dates too. After a few months, you will be pleasantly surprised at what you have learned and how many of your old feelings and attitudes have changed.

If you take the time to learn and practice the techniques and record your progress, you are on the way to conquering your speech anxiety. It will be one of the best things you have ever done. Commit yourself to a personal practice schedule and to journaling. You can do it!

Journaling #5 Activity: BASICS, Firing Order, & Plan

Name   **Date**

Today in your journal, you will reflect on your firing order of personality dimensions and what you have learned about conquering speech anxiety using a personal plan. Use the following points to guide your journaling:

1. Reflect on the six BASICS personality dimensions (Behavior, Affect, Sensations, Imagery, Cognitions, Stress--biological functions and interpersonal support). For each dimension, describe where you are experiencing the most speech anxiety.

2. Picture in your mind your last public speaking experience (or an anxious time when you spoke in front of a group). List the top three dimensions in your firing order and how you experienced them.

3. Based on your firing order and matching treatment techniques, which techniques are you most looking forward to practicing? Why?

4. How will you find the time to practice the speech anxiety-reduction techniques?

5. What obstacles will you face in keeping your personal plan and practice schedule?

6. What you will do to overcome the obstacles?

Chapter Summary

The multidimensional approach to overcoming speech anxiety emphasizes the importance of matching treatment techniques to each of your seven personality dimensions. For help in remembering the personality dimensions, use the acronym BASICS: behavior, affect, sensation, imagery, cognition, and stress (stress includes biological functions and interpersonal support). Tracking the firing order refers to determining which of the BASICS dimensions fires first (initiates speech anxiety). Applying treatment to the first dimension in your firing order is like stopping the lead domino in a snake-like chain of dominoes from falling; it lessens the impact on the other dimensions and impedes speech anxiety at its initiating point.

Once you have determined your firing order, you will select techniques to match each of the dimensions involved. Skills training targets the behavior dimension. Systematic desensitization (SD) and deep abdominal breathing target the affect and sensation dimensions. SD and mental rehearsal (also called visualization) target the imagery dimension. Cognitive restructuring and mental rehearsal target the cognitive dimension. Interpersonal support, physical exercise, and stress-reduction programs target the stress (drugs/biological functions and interpersonal relationships) dimension.

To conquer your speech anxiety, you will need to develop a personal plan and practice schedule. Start by committing yourself to your goal, then actively learn the techniques and practice them following a schedule. In addition, you will need to keep a journal of your thoughts and progress; journaling is one more aid that can help you restructure your thinking and manage physical and psychological stresses. If you take the time to follow your plan to conquer your speech anxiety, it will be one of the best things you have ever done.

Review

After reading this chapter, you should be able to answer the following:

1. Explain the multidimensional approach to conquering speech anxiety.

2. What does the acronym BASICS represent?

3. Define "tracking the firing order."

4. What is the purpose of tracking the firing order of dimensions involved in your speech anxiety?

5. List the personality dimensions in the BASICS acronym and the techniques targeted to each dimension.

6. Explain which dimension is at the top of your firing order, how you determined your firing order, and what technique you will use first.

7. Based on what you read in this chapter, which technique do you believe will be the most helpful to you? Why?

8. Describe how you will find the time to practice the techniques and how much time you will plan for the techniques each week.

9. Explain the benefits of keeping a journal and when you started keeping one.

Notes

[1]Allen, Hunter, & Donohue, 1989; Ayres & Hopf, 1993; Dwyer, 1995; Dwyer, 2000; Rossi & Seiler, 1989; Whitworth & Cochran, 1996

[2]Lazarus, 1989, 1997

[3]Lazarus, 1989

[4]Lazarus, 1978, p. 8

[5]Lazarus, 1989

[6]Lazarus, 1989

[7]O'Keefe, 1985

[8]Lazarus, 1989

[9]Ullrich & Lutgendorf, 2002

[10]Vano, 2002

[11]Ullrich & Lutgendorf, 2002

Personal Notes

CHAPTER SIX
Diaphragmatic Breathing

Seldom do we think about the way that we breathe. It is so automatic, we take it for granted. However, breathing patterns do change in relationship to the tensions we carry. For example, if you are anxious or nervous, your breathing will tend to be rapid and shallow, and occur high in your chest. If you are relaxed, your breathing will tend to be slow and deep, and be centered in your abdomen or midsection.

6.1 Diaphragmatic Breathing Induces Relaxation

Diaphragmatic breathing is deep breathing that targets the affect and sensation dimensions of your personality. It has been shown to significantly reduce public speaking anxiety when practiced prior to giving a speech.[1] You will use diaphragmatic breathing as a first step in quieting the fight-flight-freeze response and as a way to reduce excessive activation. It also can serve as an important first step in other speech anxiety–reduction techniques.

Diaphragmatic breathing calms emotions and the physical sensations of excessive activation. It stimulates your parasympathetic nervous system, the branch of your autonomic nervous system that promotes calm feelings and tranquility and thus, triggers relaxation and shuts down the fight-flight-freeze response.

Diaphragmatic breathing uses your full lung capacity and is essential for good mental and physical health. It increases the oxygen supply to your brain and muscles. It improves concentration and can help calm a racing mind. On the other hand, shallow breathing contributes to feelings of anxiety and fatigue because it uses poorly oxygenated blood

Hyperventilation which can be reduced by diaphragmatic breathing includes symptoms such as a rapid, pounding heartbeat, shortness of breath, dizziness, and tingly sensations in your limbs. Hyperventilation involves breathing rapidly and exhaling too much carbon dioxide in relation to the amount of oxygen in your bloodstream.[2] It can occur when you are overly anxious and thus, you over-breath through your mouth. When you breathe out too much carbon dioxide, you cause (1) your heart to pump harder and faster, (2) your blood vessels to constrict, resulting in feelings of dizziness or disorientation, and (3) your nerve cells to increase alkalinity, eliciting those jittery feelings.

Fortunately, it is possible to change your breathing patterns. You can learn diaphragmatic breathing to reduce your anxiety, prevent hyperventilation, promote calmness, and improve concentration. An initial step in controlling your breathing is to become aware of it. Go to Exercise 6.1 to evaluate your breathing.

Exercise 6.1: Breathing Evaluation

Name   **Date**

Take a moment right now to evaluate your breathing. You will need to sit back in a chair (with your knees bent and your head, shoulders, and neck relaxed) OR lie down on a flat surface or bed (with your knees bent, your head supported, and your arms resting comfortably at your sides). Next, concentrate on your breathing for about a minute. Now place one hand on your abdomen just below your rib cage and the other hand on your upper chest. Concentrate on the location that rises and falls as you breathe. Then, answer each of the following questions.

1. Does your breathing occur high in your chest (your chest rises when you breathe)?
   Yes   No

2. Does your breathing go deep down into your abdomen (your abdomen rises when you breathe)? Yes   No

3. Is your breathing rapid? Yes   No

4. Is your breathing slow and relaxed? Yes   No

5. Have you noticed any changes in your breathing patterns when you feel anxious or stressed? Yes   No

6. Write a sentence to summarize your breathing as you have evaluated it.

Figure 6.1

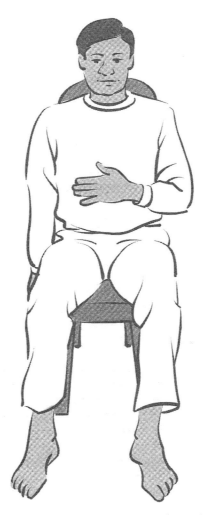

Breathing Evaluation: Place hand where breathing occurs. (Does your breathing occur high in your chest or deep down in your abdomen?)

If you evaluated your breathing as rapid, shallow, or centered in your upper chest, you probably are not making good use of the lower part of your lungs. However, be encouraged because now you have identified a problem you can change. Your breathing can become relaxing, diaphragmatic breathing that makes full use of your lung capacity. You can even learn to control it in stressful situations, such as right before you give a speech.

6.2 The Diaphragmatic Breathing Technique

For the mp3 download, see: www.iconquerspeechanxiety.com

Diaphragmatic breathing can also be called "belly breathing" or "deep abdominal breathing." This book uses the term "diaphragmatic breathing" because it is the technique so named and investigated in health and medical research. The diaphragm is the dome shaped muscle at the base of your lungs and is the most effective and efficient muscle for breathing. If you practice diaphragmatic breathing correctly, your abdomen under you diaphragm will rise and you will experience the calming benefit.[3]

Learning to breathe deeply from your abdomen is one of the first steps you can take to reduce the tenseness and physical symptoms of speech anxiety. Practicing just five minutes of diaphragmatic breathing daily can bring on moderate relaxation and produce a calming effect, opposite of the fight-flight-freeze effect.[4]

Diaphragmatic breathing is an important initial step in the systematic desensitization and mental rehearsal techniques that you will learn more about in Chapters Eight and Nine of this book. In addition, it is an excellent "quick fix" you can use to calm yourself in any tense situation. It can be easily practiced, unnoticed by anyone, while you are waiting your turn to give a speech.

By learning and practicing diaphragmatic breathing, you can reduce public speaking anxiety prior to giving a speech. In fact, recent research has shown that when individuals enrolled in a public speaking course seriously practiced about three to five minutes of diaphragmatic breathing prior to giving a speech, they reported significantly less public speaking anxiety than those enrolled in the same course but who learned only public speaking skills.[5] Since it difficult to be tense and breathe deeply at the same time, you will be able to reduce tension in your body anytime with this breathing method.[6] Follow the steps in Exercise 6.2 to practice diaphragmatic breathing.

Jon (biochemist), age 36, said: "I could never calm myself before a speech to a large crowd until I discovered I was shallow breathing from my chest. Once I tried the diaphragmatic breathing method, I started to relax before a presentation. It was a turning point in my life and the nervousness I always felt about giving a presentation … diaphragmatic breathing really works."

Exercise 6.2: Practice Diaphragmatic Breathing

You can train yourself to use diaphragmatic breathing by practicing this exercise daily for about five minutes at a time. You can choose to sit or stand during the exercise. Try not to lie down because if you do, you could fall asleep and miss the practice session! Follow these steps:

1. Position yourself for practice.

   a. Sit back in a chair (with your knees bent and your head, shoulders, and neck relaxed) OR stand in a relaxed position. Scan your body and note if you feel any tension or anxiety.

   b. Place one hand directly below your rib cage—that is your abdomen—and the other hand on your upper chest. You should be able to feel your diaphragm move as you breathe.

2. Practice slow complete exhaling first.

   a. Breathe in through your nose, if possible.

   b. Now, pucker your lips and make a slow soft "whoooo" sound like you were blowing out a few birthday candles. (In your mind, you should be able to count slowly to six.)

   c. Take a regular breath in and out.

   d. Then practice exhaling slowly and completely three or four more times so that when you exhale your hand on your abdomen falls inward (i.e., goes DOWN). When you have exhaling down then you are ready to put it all together.

3. Practice the four steps of diaphragmatic breathing.

a. Inhale slowly and deeply through your nose so that your stomach moves (i.e., abdomen expands against your hand). As you do this, count slowly to four (1—2—3—4). The hand on your chest should remain still or barely move.

b. Pause slightly and smile while you again count slowly to four (1—2—3—4). (Smiling releases endorphins— the natural mood elevators into your blood.)

c. Exhale slowly through your mouth and tighten your stomach muscles so they fall inward while you breathe out. Remember to pucker your lips and make a slow soft "whoooo" sound like you are blowing out a candle. In your mind, try to count twice as long as you did when you inhaled. Your hand on your upper chest should remain still.

d. Relax and take a normal breath or two. Let your muscles go loose and limp as you make an effort to let all the tension drain away from every part of your body. Continue taking at least ten to fifteen deep diaphragmatic breaths with slow, full exhales. It will take about five minutes, but try to work up to 10 minutes per day to experience the full anxiety-reduction benefits of diaphragmatic breathing.

Note: When you practice this technique, try to keep your breathing smooth and regular. Try not to gulp the air. If you get a little lightheaded at first, from the increased supply of oxygen, simply return to a regular breathing pattern for a minute or two and the lightheadedness will subside.

Keep Practicing! You will want to practice this technique every day for at least two weeks. In this way, you will train your body to master the technique. Once you have practiced, you will find it an indispensable tool to use whenever you feel anxious or tense. Diaphragmatic breathing will trigger relaxation and especially help you feel calm right before you give a speech. You can adjust the exercise so it can be performed without others noticing. Simply follow the same procedures, except exhale slowly and fully through your mouth without making the wind sound or even exhale through your nose.

Figure 6.2 Diaphragmatic Breathing

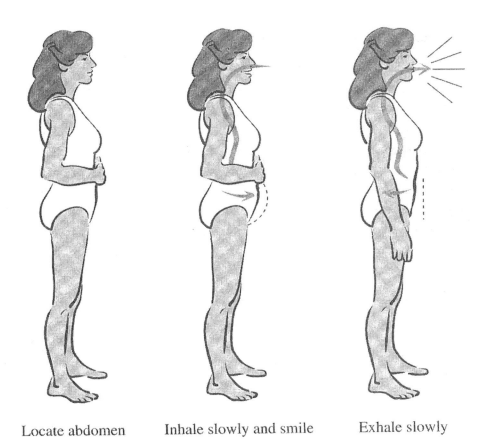

Locate abdomen   Inhale slowly and smile   Exhale slowly

6.3 The Calming Sigh

Beyond the basic deep abdominal breathing exercise, physicians and psychologists have suggested several breathing exercises to reduce stress. One quick breathing exercise that has been helped many relieve tension while preparing for a speech is called the "Calming Sigh." It takes only a minute and can easily be practiced while you are getting ready for a speech, driving to work, or traveling to give a presentation.

One of the signs that you are not getting enough oxygen or are experiencing a lot of physical tension is your body's desire to sigh or yawn.[7]   A sigh is your body's way of relaxing and releasing tension. The Calming Sigh exercise can help relieve feelings of tension and nervousness. It includes inhaling a deep abdominal breath and then softly sighing on the exhale. Follow the Calming Sigh directions in Exercise 6.3.

Exercise 6.3: Practice the Calming Sigh

Name   **Date**

The Calming Sigh is an easy breathing exercise that helps trigger relaxation and reduce feelings of tension or nervousness. It is like a quiet yawn that gently opens the air passages.

Follow these steps:

1. Sitting or standing, inhale slowly and deeply through your nose, feeling your abdomen expand.

2. Now, simply sigh ("ahhhhh") gently, softly, and deeply. Let the air flow naturally out of your lungs. Be sure to exhale slowly and completely while sighing.

3. Then, tell your body to go limp and to RELAX.

4. Continue to practice the Calming Sigh for five or more times.

5. Now describe your CA level after practicing the Calming Sigh.

The Calming Sigh can be used anytime you feel tense. You might find it helpful to practice it before you start the diaphragmatic breathing exercise. Many people have reported that practicing the Calming Sigh first and then following it with the diaphragmatic breathing is an especially good tension-reduction routine to use immediately before delivering a speech.

Journaling #6 Activity: Diaphragmatic Breathing Analysis

Name   **Date**

Today in your journal, summarize what you have learned about your breathing and what you will do to change your breathing to help reduce tension, anxiety, and nervousness. Use the following points to guide your journaling:

1. Sit back in a chair (with your knees bent and your head, shoulders, and neck relaxed), and your arms resting comfortably at your sides). Now, describe your breathing pattern (e.g., slow relaxed in your abdomen, rapid, shallow, high in your chest).

2. Again, sit back in your chair and practice the steps in Exercise 6.2, Diaphragmatic Breathing for five minutes. Now describe your breathing pattern and how you feel.

3. Contrast your before and after feelings. In other words, contrast what you wrote about your breathing pattern in question #1 above (before practicing diaphragmatic breathing) with what you wrote about your breathing pattern in question #2 (after practicing diaphragmatic breathing). In other words, describe the effect the diaphragmatic breathing has on your body and its potential to help reduce tension before you give a speech.

4. Practice the Calming Sigh five times. Be sure to combine a diaphragmatic inhaling breath with a slow, calm exhale. Now, with your eyes closed, visualize a situation where you would like to speak in public. Hold that situation in your mind and practice five more calming sighs. Describe how your body feels after sighing.

5. Describe your CA level after practicing diaphragmatic breathing and the Calming Sigh.

Chapter Summary

Diaphragmatic breathing targets the affect and sensation dimensions of your personality. It can calm your emotions and the physiological sensations of excessive activation, improve your concentration, and reduce the symptoms of hyperventilation. This deep abdominal breathing exercise is a quick fix you can use anytime you feel tense. Also, it is the initial step in both the systematic desensitization and the mental rehearsal techniques presented in later chapters. You can train yourself to use diaphragmatic breathing by practicing the exercise about five minutes per day for two weeks. The Calming Sigh is a breathing exercise that releases tension and is especially helpful in preparation for delivering a speech.

Review

After reading this chapter, you should be able to answer the following:

1. Which personality dimensions are targeted by the diaphragmatic breathing technique?

2. Explain hyperventilation and how to stop its symptoms.

3. List the benefits of practicing the diaphragmatic breathing exercise.

4. What innate response does diaphragmatic breathing exercise shut down?

5. How can you train yourself in diaphragmatic breathing?

6. Explain how to practice the Calming Sigh.

7. How can you train yourself in diaphragmatic breathing?

8. Now that you have experienced diaphragmatic breathing and the Calming Sigh, explain how these techniques have helped you relax and relieve tension in your body.

Notes

[1]Howe & Dwyer, 2007

[2]Bourne, 2005

[3]Bourne, 2005; Seaward, 1998

[4]Greenberg, 2003; Seaward, 1998

[5]German et al., 2003, Davidson & Dwyer, 2007

[6]Davidson & Dwyer, 2007

[7]Davis, M., Eshelman, E. & McKay, M., 2000

[8]McKay, M., Davis, M., Davis, M., Eshelman, E., Fanning, P., 2008

CHAPTER SEVEN
Cognitive Reconstruction

7.1 Cognitive Restructuring Adjusts Thinking

Cognitive restructuring is a well-researched "cognitive modification" technique that targets the affect and sensation personality dimensions.[1] It is based on the premise that anxiety and nervousness are generated when you think anxious and negative thoughts about yourself and your behavior.[2] Thus, the goal of this technique is to help you modify or change your thinking in order to change your nervous feelings. Cognitive restructuring targets the cognitive dimension of your personality.

The term "cognitive restructuring" (CR) is a well-chosen term to describe this technique. Cognitive refers to cognitions (i.e., your thoughts), and restructuring means to systematically rebuild or remake. Thus, cognitive restructuring, when applied to public speaking, means you will learn to rebuild your thoughts about public speaking and yourself as the speaker. By using this technique, you can change your worrisome, anxious thinking to truthful affirming statements that will help you think positively about giving a speech. This technique involves four steps, which can significantly reduce your nervousness and anxiety about public speaking.

Cognitive restructuring (CR) involves FOUR steps:

1. **Create an ultimate fears or worries list. Create a list of your worrisome self-talk and negative thoughts about public speaking.**

2. **Identify the irrational beliefs and must thoughts. Recognize and classify your ultimate fears and worries as irrational conclusions and distortions based on "must thinking."**

3. **Create positive coping statements. Develop a list of true statements to replace your irrational beliefs and must thinking.**

4. **Practice. Practice your new coping statements until they automatically replace your old must thinking and irrational beliefs.**

The first important step in the cognitive restructuring technique is to discover your anxious thoughts about public speaking so you can change them. In order to accomplish this step, you need to develop your own "Ultimate Worries List" about public speaking. Please follow the directions for Exercise 7.1 before you read any further. DO NOT SKIP THIS EXERCISE. It is an essential step in helping you learn the cognitive restructuring technique.

Exercise 7.1A: Create an Ultimate Worries List

Name   Date

In the space below, list your worries, fears, and negative thoughts about delivering a speech. Later in this chapter you will be using *Your Ultimate Worries List to* create positive coping statements. So please, complete this list carefully. To help you get started, imagine that you have just been assigned to give a speech to a large group of people and then answer these questions. (See the example of *Kim's Ultimate Worries List* on the next page.)

1. What worrisome, anxious, or nervous thoughts do you have about giving the speech (e.g., I worry I will make a mistake and the audience will think I am stupid)?

2. What negative self-statements do you say to yourself (e.g., I know I am going to make a fool of myself)?

3. What is the worst thing that you could imagine would happen?

4. Please use your answers from above to complete the following *7.1B: My Ultimate Worries Public Speaking Chart.*

Exercise 7.1B: My Ultimate Worries Public Speaking Chart

Worry #1	
Worry #2	
Worry #3	
Worry #4	
Worry #5	
Worry #6	
Worry #7	
Worry #8	
Worry #9	
Worry #10	

Example: Kim's Ultimate Worries

Worry #1	*I will make a mistake or forget something; my speech will be ruined. I will be embarrassed and look stupid.*
Worry #2	*Everyone is staring at me and judging everything I do and say. I can't stand it.*
Worry #3	*I can't sound eloquent and smooth so I will look foolish.*
Worry #4	*Everyone will see me blush or shake or hear my voice crack when I get nervous. They will poke fun of me.*
Worry #5	*I worry about giving a speech for days in advance and doing a poor job.*
Worry #6	*I hate to feel nervous, You have to feel calm to be a good speaker.*
Worry #7	*The audience will think my speech is boring or that I am ignorant.*
Worry #8	*I will speak so fast the audience won't be able to understand me.*
Worry #9	*When I feel anxious, I could lose control or faint from the anxiety.*
Worry #10	*I am afraid someone will ask a question I can't answer. When I can't answer, some will think I am dumb.*

(TEAR-OUT PAGE FOR PRACTICE AND STUDY)

7.2   *Identify Irrational Beliefs and Must Thoughts*

The second step in cognitive restructuring is to identify the irrational beliefs and must thoughts on your Ultimate Worries List. These beliefs include negative, illogical, and unproductive thoughts or unrealistic demands you place on yourself. You will soon find out that these irrational beliefs can be at the center of your nervousness and anxiety.

Irrational Beliefs vs. Rational Beliefs

Cognitive psychologists tell us that the cause of anxiety and irrational fear is often our irrational beliefs. Irrational beliefs are evaluative thoughts that are rigid and stymieing. They keep you from reaching your goals. Irrational beliefs are illogical and unrealistic because they are not related to a personal harm or a truly perilous event.[3] They are unproductive beliefs because they keep you from achieving your goals and purposes.

In contrast, rational beliefs are logical and realistic beliefs that help you achieve your goals. Rational beliefs involve concern for the well-being of yourself and others, but they are not immobilizing.[4] Instead, they motivate you to engage in self-enhancing behaviors. For example, rational concern or rational non-immobilizing fear causes you to take shelter when you hear a tornado warning or to protect your car when you hear a potential hail storm is approaching. Rational concern leads you to discourage a friend from driving when he or she has been drinking. Rational concern about losing a joy or failing an important exam causes you to work hard or set aside enough time to study so you can earn a good grade. It just makes sense to be concerned about potential danger or loss or injury. The human emotion of concern is crucial to your survival and part of your basic nature.

Concern becomes an anxious problem when it turns into irrational, immobilizing fear and anxiety.[5] Irrational fearful thoughts are at the core of your public speaking anxiety; you are projecting harm and danger into a situation that is neither harmful nor dangerous. Although you may feel fearful and anxious about public speaking, logically, there is no potential danger. If you think about it, have you ever heard of anyone getting killed or dropping dead from giving a speech? Public speaking is not a perilous life threatening event! It is only your irrational beliefs about public speaking that are causing you fear, worry, anxiety, and nervousness.

The ABCDs of Irrational Fear and Anxiety[6]

The ABCDs of irrational fear and anxiety can further teach you that irrational beliefs are at the heart of your speech anxiety. In addition the ABCD's will help you learn how you can begin to understand and to stop your fearful beliefs that initiate you speech anxiety.

A	Stands for the Activating Event, like public speaking, that arouses or activates your fear, anxiety, and nervousness.
B	Stands for your Beliefs (irrational fearful beliefs) about the activating event.
C	Stands for the Consequences (emotional consequences like anxiety, fear, or nervousness) you feel about the Activating Event.
D	Stands for Disconnecting the irrational, fearful beliefs about the Activating Event (public speaking) in order to eliminate your Consequences of anxiety, fear, and resulting nervousness.

It is not the A=Activating event that causes the C=Consequences of nervousness and anxiety. Otherwise, everyone would feel the same about the same event. But they don't! For example, why is it that one individual feels that giving a speech is a fun, invigorating, and enjoyable experience while another individual feels it is a dreadful nerve-wracking occasion to be avoided? Why would one person describe those "feelings" as "awful and immobilizing" while another person describes the activation as "energizing?"

The event of public speaking does not cause the fear, anxiety, and nervousness or both individuals would feel the same. It is the B=Beliefs about the event that cause one individual to feel anxious or fearful while another individual feels enthused and happy. If you want to get rid of your anxiety, fears, and nervousness about public speaking, you will need to Disconnect (change) your irrational beliefs. So the ABCDs is an important acronym you can use to remind yourself to D=Disconnect your irrational beliefs in order to eliminate your anxieties and nervousness.

Irrational Beliefs Are Based on Must Thinking

Research in the communication field reports that anxiety about public speaking often includes irrational beliefs such as:

> "My audience will be evaluating every word I say and every little detail about me so I must give a perfect performance. I must never make a mistake."

These irrational beliefs are called "MUST THOUGHTS." Must thoughts are all the unrealistic things you tell yourself you MUST do that can disturb your work and your life.[7] All the perfectionist demands you tell yourself fit into the "must thoughts" or "must thinking" category. They include all the "shoulds," "ought tos," "have "tos," and "musts" you demand of yourself, others, and your life situations. They often result in more negative self-talk and distorted thinking. They are responsible for your anxiety and nervousness about public speaking. To help you identify your public speaking must thoughts in an effort to change them, please complete Exercise 7.2.

Exercise 7.2: My Must Thoughts and Unrealistic Demands

Name   **Date**

1. Do you think MUST THOUGHTS ABOUT YOURSELF? Must thoughts about yourself, as a public speaker, may include the following perfectionist demands you place on yourself. <u>Please check (√)</u> all of the MUST THOUGHTS that apply to you in a public speaking situation.

    a. I must say just the right thing.

    b. I must never make a mistake.

    c. I must make a terrific impression.

    d. I must be perfect.

    e. I must always appear completely in control and sound intelligent.

    f. If I say the wrong thing, make a mistake, or look nervous, it will be awful, I won't be able to bear it, I will look like a fool.

    g. I will look incompetent and incapable.

2. Do you think MUST THOUGHTS ABOUT OTHERS? Must thoughts about others in the public speaking include any perfectionist demands you think about your **audience.** <u>Please check (√)</u> all of the MUST THOUGHTS that apply to you in a public speaking situation.

    a. Everyone must like me.

    b. Everyone must like what I have to say.

    c. Everyone should be enthusiastic and never bored.

    d. Everyone must give me an excellent evaluation if I speak.

    e. If everyone doesn't like me or if anyone looks bored or disinterested, I will be a failure.

3. Do you think MUST THOUGHTS ABOUT PUBLIC SPEAKING SITUATIONS? Must thoughts about public speaking many include any of these perfectionist thoughts you demand of the **situations** when you speak. Again, <u>please check</u> (√) all of the MUST THOUGHTS that apply to you in a public speaking situation.

    a. The situation must be perfect.

    b. I must know everything about the topic.

    c. If I don't know absolutely everything about the topic or if I feel nervous, I MUST NOT speak.

    d. Since public speaking is an awful situation, I MUST AVOID IT.

    e. I might do something stupid and look like an idiot.

(TEAR-OUT PAGE FOR PRACTICE AND STUDY)

Did you find must thoughts in Exercise 7.2? You most likely found statements that resemble your must thinking. Remember Must Thoughts are the rigid, perfectionistic, and unrealistic demands you place on yourself. They are irrational because no one can meet all of the perfectionistic must demands you place on yourself. When you cannot meet your own must demands, you give yourself and others a negative evaluation and soon generate more self-defeating thoughts. Must thoughts will give you anxiety, immobilize you, and prevent you from achieving your goals.

Rational Beliefs Use a Communication Orientation

Rational beliefs are the opposite of must thoughts because they are not dogmatic. They include desires, preferences, or wishes. Rational thoughts do not demand perfection. For example, a rational belief says: I want to give a good speech, but if I make a mistake or everyone doesn't appreciate what I have to say, or if I don't get a perfect, I will still like myself. I will have helped some people. I can be myself. I will offer what I can. I will be satisfied with doing my best.

Rational beliefs view public speaking from a communication orientation, not from a performance orientation. A communication orientation (or communication perspective) views public speaking as a relaxed communication encounter that you use daily to get your message across to others.[8] You use it all the time. A communication orientation relies on the same basic conversational delivery skills you use daily with family and friends.

Irrational Beliefs Use a Performance Orientation

Irrational Beliefs Use a Performance Orientation. A performance orientation (or performance perspective) erroneously views public speaking as something like an Olympic performance that requires formal eloquence, polished delivery, and perfection in order to be effective. This orientation views an audience as Olympic judges who are hypercritical and closely evaluate every move.[9] The performance orientation views one mistake as an unspeakable failure and one that is apt to knock out any further opportunity.

In the communication orientation, your goal is to help the audience understand your message.[10] Like everyday conversation, you use the same natural conversational style that you do when talking to a respected friend. You can be yourself; you do NOT have to be perfect.

A communication orientation views an audience as fellow members of the human race. They are not hypercritical or one gigantic ear waiting to criticize you for the least mistake. Members of your audience are like you when you listen to a speaker. They want to hear the message; they want the best for you. They are not judging every word you speak. They are simply looking for ideas to help them in some way or to enrich their lives.

A rational belief about public speaking includes a communication orientation, not a performance orientation. A rational belief is NOT dogmatic or perfectionistic about yourself, your delivery, or your audience.

7.3 Must Thoughts Lead to Irrational Conclusions

Rational beliefs and a communication orientation lead to different conclusions than irrational beliefs and a performance orientation. Rational beliefs are flexible, do not demand perfection, and do not escalate into dogmatic musts. Instead they help you reach your goals.[11] On the other hand, irrational beliefs involve *must thinking* that demands perfection, which is impossible for any human being to achieve. In addition, *must thinking* leads to irrational conclusions that heighten fear, anxiety, and nervousness.

Irrational conclusions are stymieing and keep you from reaching your goals or from devising new ones. Irrational conclusions can be understood with the terms "awfulizing," "I-can't-stand-it-itus," "damnation thinking," and "always-and-never thinking."[12]

Irrational Conclusions

The following four irrational conclusions are related to public speaking anxiety:

Awfulizing means you determine some event is 100 percent awful, terrible, and appalling.

I-can't-stand-it-itus means you conclude a particular event is so horrible that you cannot endure it or tolerate it.

Damnation thinking means you excessively criticize yourself and believe you are a "damnable person" because you cannot live up to the perfection you expect or you think the audience expects.

Always-and-never thinking means you insist on absolutes and conclude that situations will always be the same; they will never change, and past experiences will always predict the future.

To help you identify your irrational conclusions about public speaking, please complete Exercise 7.3:

Exercise 7.3: My Irrational Conclusions

Name   **Date**

As you read through the following questions and descriptions, please <u>circle</u> the name of each of the irrational conclusions that you have about public speaking.

1. **Do you practice awfulizing?** Do you believe that public speaking is 100 percent awful, ad, and terrible? Do you rate it as one of the worst things you could ever have to do? If you do, you are awfulizing from the must thoughts you demand of yourself.

2. **Do you have I-can't-stand-it-itus?** Do you believe public speaking is so horrible that you can NOT endure it? Do you believe that you can find NO happiness whatsoever if you have to give a speech? If you do, you have developed I-can't-stand-itus toward public speaking.

3. **Do you engage in damnation thinking?** Do you excessively criticize yourself or others? Instead of admitting that you are a fallible human who can make a mistake, do you label yourself as stupid or worthless because you can't give a flawless speech? Instead of acknowledging that not everyone will like you, do you damn yourself or your audience because some people might not appreciate your speech, interests, or ideas? If you do, you have developed damnation thinking about yourself and others.

4. **Do you employ always-and-never thinking?** Do you believe you will never become a good public speaker? Do you predict that you will always forget some part of your speech because you did in the past? Do you tell yourself that you will always be an incompetent speaker? If you do, you have developed always-and-never thinking about yourself and your future.

7.4 Must Thoughts Lead to Cognitive Distortions

The four irrational conclusions--**awfulizing, I-can't-stand-it-itus, damnation thinking,** and **always-and-never-thinking**--are linked to nervousness, anxiety, and goal defeat. They will not enhance your behavior or help you meet challenges head on, but instead they will spiral into more negative self-talk and cognitive distortions.

Cognitive distortions are erroneous and negative thoughts.[13] These erroneous thoughts include negative self-statements and self-put-downs that sway your thoughts away from relishing positive experiences. Cognitive distortions about public speaking include **peephole thinking** (focusing on mistakes or negatives while ignoring the positives), **psychic reading** (predicting you will do poorly or others will not like you or your speech), **microscopic viewing** (blowing up the importance of a speech to gigantic proportions), **emotional reasoning** (calling all feelings of activation "bad" and a sign that a speech will go badly), **all-or-nothing categorizing** (classifying one mistake in a speech as total disaster or failure), **performance demanding** (believing you must become formal or something other than yourself to be an effective speaker), **personalizing** (taking everything personally; if someone laughs, talks, or is sleepy, you think it is about you), and **perfectionizing** (believing you must be perfect in every way, look perfect, and give a perfect speech to be an effective speaker). To help you identify your cognitive distortions about public speaking in an effort to change them, please complete Exercise 7.4.

Exercise 7.4: My Cognitive Distortions List

Name   **Date**

As you read through the following descriptions, please check (√) OR circle the cognitive distortions that you have about public speaking. Then remind yourself of the truth by reading The Truth statement aloud to yourself.

1. **Peephole thinking** means you focus on one negative detail (like you would peep through a peephole in a door), to the exclusion of all other information. For example, you may receive many positive comments about a speech or topic, but you focus on the one small point you forgot or the mistake you once made.

    The Truth: Directing your attention to positive messages and to presenting your message will help you reach your speaking goals. Although you can learn from constructive suggestions, you need not focus on past mistakes, shortcomings, fears or the negative criticism that others once gave you.

2. **Psychic reading** means you anticipate the worst outcome and try to predict what others are thinking. For example, you say to yourself, "I will never give a good speech, no one will like what I have to say, and I know I will forget some part of my speech or make a mistake." You might notice an audience member yawning, who in reality has worked all night or crammed for an exam, but as a psychic reader, you falsely presume, "My audience member is bored and uninterested in my speech."

    The Truth: You cannot predict the future or read another's mind. If someone yawns, she is sleepy. If you prepare your speech outline, you will have notes to guide you. If you forget a point, you can refer to your notes and keep going.

3. **Microscopic viewing** means you look at a speech as an enormous, even gargantuan event, as if it were a tiny insect enlarged to gigantic proportions under the view of a microscope. In reality, it is minuscule and occupies only a pencil dot on the line of your life. For example, you might worry for days about delivering a five or ten-minute speech as if it were a monstrous task. In reality, it is like a dust mite invisible to the naked eye, but you have enlarged it to look huge as could happen when viewing the dust mite under a microscope.

   The Truth: Giving a speech occupies only a very short time in your life span. Worrying about giving a speech exaggerates its importance and takes away from the time you could spend preparing.

4. **Emotional reasoning** means you rely on feelings to determine the facts. For example, you think: "I can feel myself getting nervous--that's a sign that it will be a terrible speech and I will get a poor evaluation."

   The Truth: A little activation is normal and a sign you are alive. Everyone experiences some activation. It can get you "psyched up" and add to your enthusiasm. It should not determine your thoughts. It is not a sign that you have lost control. Focusing on your message instead of your nervousness will help your nervous feelings subside. Preparing, organizing, and practicing your speech will help you get good feedback.

5. **All-or-nothing categorizing** means you believe it is a perfect speech or else it is a bad speech. You think that if you make a mistake your entire speech will be a disaster or failure. For example, you might think: "If I forget something or don't say just the right thing or make a mistake, it will be a catastrophe. People will judge my speech as terrible and I will be a failure."

   The Truth: Even the most experienced speakers make mistakes or overlook points. Your message can be effective, even if it is not perfect. Even the best speakers make mistakes, correct themselves, and keep going.

6. **Performance demanding** means you believe in the performance orientation. You think you must become something other than yourself to be an effective speaker. You think, "I must have perfect, formal, flawless, eloquent delivery. I can't be myself." Others are rating me as if I am in an Olympic competition.

The Truth: Public speaking relies on communication skills that you use in everyday conversation. Your focus will be on helping the audience understand your message. You can be yourself and use your natural delivery skills. Even the most experienced speakers are NOT perfect. Your speech can be effective and help others, even if it is not perfect.

7. **Personalizing means** you take everything personally. If someone is overly critical toward you, their criticism says more about them than about you. For example, while speaking, you notice two people laughing and you conclude: "They are laughing at me; I must look like a fool." If someone excessively criticizes you, it may be a function of his or her personality or attitude, but you take it personally for years to come.

The Truth: You cannot base your opinion of yourself on what others do or say. Some will like you and your speech topic and be interested, others may not. Just make the effort to prepare and offer what you can. You have a right to express your ideas and be who you are. Your evaluation of yourself does not depend on the critical words or behaviors of others.

8. **Perfectionizing means** you believe you must look perfect and never make a mistake in order to be acceptable. For example, you think: "No one should ever see me sweat, stumble, shake, or blush. If I cannot look really good or give a perfect speech, I will be an embarrassment."

The Truth: No one will ever be perfect in this life. We are all fallible humans who make mistakes. You can accept yourself. Your audience cannot feel your heartbeat and will NOT notice the nervousness you feel. They are simply listening for helpful ideas. Accept yourself.

How many of the distortions apply to you? Three? Four? Five? All of them? When you think must thoughts that demand perfection of yourself, you will irrationally believe that your audience requires perfection in order to appreciate your speech. Your thoughts will be flooded with irrational conclusions, cognitive distortions, and more negative self-statements.

7.5 Develop Positive Coping Statements

The third step in cognitive restructuring is to create a list of truthful coping statements to replace your old worries and irrational beliefs about public speaking. Once you have discovered your ultimate worries about public speaking and identified them as irrational beliefs (including must thoughts, irrational conclusions, and cognitive distortions), then you are ready for this next step.

Exercise 7.5 will help you begin to replace your irrational beliefs with positive coping statements. Please read through a list of positive coping statements and then check the ones that apply most to your worries and distortions about public speaking.

Exercise 7.5: A Checklist of Positive Coping Statements
Name   **Date**

As you read through the following coping statements, please place a check (√) beside the statements that apply to your ***must thinking, cognitive distortions,*** or ***irrational conclusions*** about public speaking.

1. Public speaking is a communication encounter, NOT a magnified performance. My goal is to clearly communicate my message. I can use the same conversational style I use daily with family and friends. I can be myself.

2. Because I am able to speak without nervousness in many situations involving my friends or family, I can learn to speak without nervousness in front of any individual, most of who experience the anxiety about public speaking just as I do.

3. My audience is NOT evaluating every word or every hair on my head. Fellow humans, like me, are simply looking for helpful ideas to enrich their lives in some way. As I focus on helping them, they will be supportive.

4. Worry only agitates and demoralizes a person. I have no need to worry about my speech because I will contribute something by planning and sharing my ideas. Preparation and organization contribute the most to earning respect and receiving good feedback.

5. Audiences seldom notice nervousness; they can't feel my heart beat. Focusing on my fears or feelings of nervousness will only prevent me from concentrating on my presentation. I will direct my attention to communicating the ideas in my speech.

6. No one is perfect in all aspects of life. I do not have to be perfect or give a perfect speech. I only have to give my best effort.

7. If I lose my place in my speech or forget something, it is not a disaster. Most people won't notice. My audience friends will wait while I look at my notes and move on to my next point. Even the best speakers make mistakes or skip sections, and go on.

8. If I research my topic and prepare my speech, I will sound knowledgeable. I will probably know more about the topic than most people in my audience. My enthusiasm will be contagious and interest others in the topic.

9. Blaming myself for past shortcomings or failures will NOT help me. Learning positive coping statements to replace negative thinking WILL help reduce my speech anxiety and nervousness.

10. Even if I feel some anxiety, I will act as if I am NOT anxious. I will believe in myself and my goals to help others.

11. I have coped with hard tasks or difficulties in my life so I can cope with the challenge of public speaking. In fact, I am committed to meeting this challenge.

12. Dreading to give a speech is an extreme exaggeration of the importance that one speech has in my life. Giving a speech occupies such a small amount of time in my entire life that it could be compared to looking for a small pin dropped on an interstate highway while driving 60 miles per hour.

13. Feelings of activation when giving a speech are normal and to be expected. (Only those in a coffin no longer experience stress.) Such feelings are a sign that I am alive and enthused.

14. I will gracefully accept any positive comments and praise from others about my speech or myself. I will simply say "thank you" when I am complimented. I can focus on the positive in my life and appreciate my achievements.

7.6 Personalize Your Coping Statements.

For an mp3 download, see: www.iconquerspeechanxiety.com

Now is the time to systematically modify or rebuild your thoughts. In this next exercise, you will develop your own personal coping statements by using or combining any copying statements on the previous list in Exercise 7.5 and putting them into your own words. It is important that they become your coping statements. They need to be personal and useful to you. They should fit your list of *ultimate worries, must thoughts, cognitive distortions,* and *irrational conclusions* about public speaking. Please follow the directions in Exercise 7.6. See the following example of a Kim's Coping Statements and how they match Must Thoughts, Irrational Conclusions, and Cognitive Distortions.

Example: Kim's Coping Statement Matched to Worries

Ultimate Worries	Must Thoughts, Irrational Conclusions & Cognitive Distortions	Positive Coping Statements
1. I will make a mistake or forget something; my speech will be ruined, I will look stupid.	Peephole Thinking, Perfectionizing, & All-or-Nothing Categorizing	If I lose my place in my speech or forget something, it's not a disaster. Most people won't even notice. My audience will wait while I look at my notes. Even the best speakers make mistakes and go on.
2. Everyone is staring at me and judging me. I can't stand it.	Must Thought (everyone must like me) & Performance Orientation	The audience is NOT evaluating every word I say. Fellow humans are looking for helpful ideas to enrich their lives. Most will be supportive.
3. I have to sound eloquent and smooth or I will look foolish.	Performance Demanding	I can be myself. My main goal is to communicate my message. I can be conversational like I am daily with family and friends.
4. I will blush, shake or my voice crack. They will laugh at me.	Damnation Thinking & Perfectionizing	Audiences don't notice nervousness; they can't feel my heart beat. Focusing on my nervousness will take away from my concentration. I will focus on communicating the ideas in my speech.

5. I worry about giving a speech for days in advance. I could do a bad job or get a poor evaluation.	Microscopic Viewing & Psychic Reading	Worry will not help me. Giving a speech occupies such a small amount of time in my entire life that it can be compared to looking for a small pin dropped on an interstate highway. I will not worry because I will plan and research my topic. Preparation and organization will help me earn a decent feedback.
6. I hate to feel nervous; it means a bad speech. It's awful. I should feel calm to be a good speaker.	Awfulizing & Emotional Reasoning	Feeling a little activation is normal. Activation is a sign I am alive and "psyched up" to give a speech.
7. The audience will think my speech is boring or that I am ignorant.	Damnation Thinking & Psychic Reading.	If I research my topic and prepare my speech, I will be prepared. I will likely know more about the topic than most in the audience. My enthusiasm will interest others in my topic.
8. As always, I will be so nervous and speak so fast the audience won't be able to understand me.	Always-and-Never Thinking & Psychic Reading	Because I am able to speak without nervousness with friends and family, I can learn to speak without nervousness in front of others who often experience the same anxiety.
9. When I feel anxious, I could lose control or faint from the anxiety.	Emotional Reasoning	Even if I feel some anxiety, I will act as if I am NOT anxious and believe in myself. I will tell myself to be confident, not nervous.
10. I am afraid someone will ask a question I can't answer. When I don't answer, they will think I am dumb.	Damnation Thinking, Personalizing, & Psychic Reading	I will gracefully accept praise from others. I will simply say "thank you" when I am complimented. If I don't know an answer to a question, I can say "I will look it up for you."
11. I hate public speaking. I don't have public speaking skills; others do a lot better than me.	I-Can't-Stand-It-Itus	I will learn public speaking skills. I do not have to give a perfect speech. I only have to do my best.

Exercise 7.6: My Coping Statements List

Name   **Date**

Please complete the following chart in order to develop your own coping statements list about public speaking. Transfer your Ultimate Worries from Exercise 7.1 to the first column in this chart. Label each worry or anxiety as a Must Thought, Cognitive Distortion or Irrational Conclusion (see Exercises 7.2, 7.3, 7.4). Then write your own coping statement for each anxious thought based on Exercise 7.5. Try to make each coping statement personal and useful to you. Do not skip this exercise. It is an essential step in conquering your anxiety and nervousness about of public speaking.

Ultimate Worries	Must Thoughts, Irrational Conclusions &Cognitive Distortions	Positive Coping Statements

(TEAR-OUT PAGE FOR PRACTICE AND STUDY)

Personal Notes

7.7 Practice Your Coping Statements

The fourth step in cognitive restructuring is to memorize and practice your coping statements so you will have a new script in your mind to replace your old irrational beliefs. Try to memorize your coping statements. When old must thoughts or distortions automatically pop into your mind, you will be ready to challenge them with new coping statements. To learn your coping statements and make them useful to you, you should:

1. **Read.** Read through your personal list of coping statements several times a day or until you know it by heart. Try to read it aloud so you feel a connection with each of your coping statements. Post your coping statements list on a mirror where you dress, on a refrigerator, or other conspicuous place where you can be reminded to read your list often. You may want to share your list of coping statements with a trusted friend who is also anxious about public speaking.

2. **Challenge.** Every time you feel anxious, nervous, or fearful about public speaking, challenge or ask yourself: "What am I thinking that caused me to feel this way?" Then, challenge the must thought, irrational conclusion, or cognitive distortion and call it a lie or twisted truth. Then repeat one of your coping statements to replace the irrational belief.

3. **Practice.** Practice your coping statements until they automatically replace your unproductive thoughts. Don't be discouraged if your old irrational beliefs and unproductive thoughts keep popping in your mind. You have been thinking some of those thoughts for a long time. It will take at least two weeks of diligent practice to disconnect automatic unproductive thoughts and irrational beliefs. So be heartened and know that your efforts will be rewarded with practice.

Kim, Finance Associate, age 31, wrote: "When I first practiced the coping statements, they sounded silly. As I put them in my own words, I was amazed at how much they helped me… It took a few weeks to stop my awfulizing and damnation thinking and to bring the coping statements to mind. But the more I kept practicing them, the more they took hold.

My nervousness about public speaking went down with every week when I practiced them. Cognitive restructuring works, if you use it and practice it."

The Four Steps in Cognitive Restructuring Will Work

If you faithfully practice these four steps in cognitive restructuring, you will notice that your nervousness and anxiety about public speaking will drastically diminish over the next few weeks:

1. **Create an ultimate worries and fears list.** Discover your anxious thoughts and create a list of your worrisome and negative self-talk about public speaking (i.e., Ultimate Worries List).

2. **Identify the irrational beliefs and must thoughts.** Identify and label the must thoughts, irrational conclusions, and cognitive distortions on your list. You will identify irrational beliefs--lies or twisted truths that you will no longer believe.

3. **Create positive coping statements.** You will develop a list of true statements to replace your irrational beliefs and must thinking. Write your coping statements so they are personal and useful to you.

4. **Practice.** Practice and memorize your coping statements until they automatically replace your old must thinking and irrational beliefs. Every time you catch yourself feeling anxious or nervous about public speaking, look for your negative self-talk, cognitive distortions, and irrational conclusions. Immediately confront those unproductive thoughts and replace them with your positive coping statements. Work at believing your coping statements more than your irrational beliefs. Set small weekly goals for speaking up in a meeting or giving a speech, where you can practice your coping statements in preparation for the speech.

Journaling #7 Activity: Coping Statements and Your Beliefs

Name   **Date**

Today in your journal, please reflect on what you have learned about replacing your irrational beliefs with coping statements. Use the following points to guide your journaling.

1. Reflect on your three worst worries or negative thoughts about public speaking. Describe how they have impacted your life.

2. Describe how your worst worries are related to irrational beliefs and must thoughts you think about yourself, your audience, and public speaking.

3. Reflect on the irrational conclusions or cognitive distortions that are feeding your worries, fears, and anxieties. Describe the ones you will work on changing.

4. Write your three coping statements from memory and then describe how each will help you replace an irrational belief.

5. Reflect on your plan for practicing the coping statements. What do you plan to do to keep the coping statements in your sight every day?

6. Describe your public speaking anxiety level after practicing the cognitive restructuring technique, especially after memorizing and using the coping statements to prepare to speak in front of others.

Chapter Summary

Cognitive restructuring targets the cognitive dimension and is based on the premise that if you change your anxious thoughts, you will change the way you feel. Because public speaking is not a potentially dangerous event, speech anxiety is an irrational fear or anxiety. The ABCDs remind us that it is your B=Beliefs (irrational beliefs) about the A=Activating event (public speaking) that causes your C=Consequences (nervousness, fear, and anxiety), not the event itself, so you must D=Disconnect the irrational beliefs about public speaking in order to eliminate the C=Consequences of anxiety, fear, and nervousness.

Irrational beliefs include must thoughts, which are the perfectionistic demands you make on yourself, others, and the situation. Must thoughts lead to irrational conclusions (i.e., **awfulizing, I-can't-stand-it-itus, damnation thinking, always-and-never thinking**) and cognitive distortions (i.e., peephole thinking, psychic reading, microscopic viewing, emotional reasoning, performance demanding, all-or-nothing categorizing, personalizing, and perfectionizing). By discovering your irrational beliefs about public speaking, identifying your distortions and irrational conclusions, and then learning new positive coping statements to replace them, your fear, anxiety, and nervousness associated with public speaking will greatly diminish with practice.

Review Questions

After reading this chapter, you should be able to answer the following:

1. Explain the premise of cognitive restructuring and which personality dimension it targets.

2. Briefly describe the four steps in the cognitive restructuring technique.

3. Compare and contrast rational beliefs with irrational beliefs. Give an example for each type.

4. Explain the ABCDs of irrational anxiety or nervousness.

5. What are must thoughts, and what do they have to do with speech anxiety?

6. Compare and contrast the communication orientation versus the performance orientation. Which orientation represents a rational belief?

7. Describe the four irrational conclusions and what impact they have on speech anxiety.

8. Briefly describe the eight cognitive distortions about public speaking.

9. Identify three coping statements that are most helpful for you.

10. Explain how to replace your old script of irrational beliefs with the new positive coping statements so that the coping statements become more automatic than your old irrational beliefs.

Notes

[1] Allen, et al, 1989, Ayres, 1988, Hopf & Ayres, 1992

[2]Meichenbaum, 1977

[3]Dryden & Ellis, 2010; Dryeen, Ellis, DiGiuseppe & Neenan, 2002

[4]Neenan, DiGiuseppe, & Dryden, 2010

[5]Ellis, 2001

[6]Dryden & Ellis, 2010

[7]Dryden & Ellis, 2010

[8]Motley, 2009; Motley & Molloy, 1994

[9]Motley, 2009; Motley & Molloy, 1994

[10]Burns, 1999, 2007; Dryden & Ellis, 2010

[11]Beck & Beck, 2011

[12] Distortions applied to public speaking are loosely based on general classifications of cognitive distortions or illogicalities suggested by Beck & Beck, 2011; Burns, 2007; Dryden & Ellis, 2010

[13] Coping statements are loosely based on rationalities suggested by Simpson, 1982

CHAPTER EIGHT
Systematic Desensitization

Systematic Desensitization[1] targets the affect, sensation, and imagery personality dimensions. It is specifically designed to reduce the excessive physical activation and tense feelings of nervousness associated with anxiety.[2] The goal of systematic desensitization is to help individuals develop a new relaxation response to an anxiety provoking event, such as public speaking. By using this technique you will learn to replace nervous feelings and excessive physical sensations, such as a pounding or rapid heartbeat, indigestion, nausea, sweating, dry mouth, trembling hands, or blushing, with feelings of calmness.

8.1 Systematic Desensitization Trains Your Body to Relax

Systematic desensitization can be abbreviated by the letters *SD* and its principles are rooted in learning theory. In educational psychology, you may have heard of the term *stimulus-response*. Ivan Pavlov, for example, trained his dogs to salivate (a response) upon hearing a bell ring (a stimulus). Upon noting that the dogs salivated when he brought their food, he began to feed the dogs while simultaneously ringing a bell. The dogs quickly learned to associate the ringing of a bell with food. Soon they salivated, without the food, as a response to the stimulus of the ringing bell. Based upon learning theory and in a similar way as Pavlov, you can train your body to respond to the stimulus (a public speaking event) with a relaxation response instead of your present anxiety or nervous response.

Systematic Desensitization (SD) involves three steps:

1. **Create a hierarchy of anxious events.** You will list instances or steps toward a public speaking goal that are arranged in order of intensity.

2. **Train your body in progressive and deep muscle relaxation**. You will train your body to completely relax so that you can differentiate between relaxation and tension.

3. **Condition your body to relax.** You will help your body learn a relaxation response to all the events on your hierarchy (see step#1) with the use of visualization. You will be creating a new stimulus-response bond of relaxation for public speaking as you systematically practice relaxation in response to each of the events you mentally visualize/picture.

In the past you may have unknowingly trained yourself to associate anxiety or nervous sensations with public speaking (i.e., you were Pavlov, and the dogs were the members of your body that learned nervousness in relationship to giving a presentation). In order to break this stimulus-response bond between public speaking and nervous sensations, you will need to learn and train your body in a new calming, relaxation response to public speaking. Through SD you can train yourself to associate relaxation with public speaking and thus create a new stimulus-response bond, just like Pavlov trained his dogs to salivate when a bell rang. The result will help shut down the fight-flight-freeze response and thus, reduce the excessive physical sensations and nervous feelings you experience about public speaking.

8.2 Systematic Desensitization Step One

The first step in learning SD is to create a sequential list of anxious events that lead to anxiety about public speaking. For example, these might include reading a book on public speaking, receiving a public speaking request or assignment, writing a speech outline, practicing a speech, waiting to give a presentation, etc.). You will need to identify specific situations in the speechmaking process that arouse your nervousness and anxiety. After listing these situations you will rank them on a 100-point scale to determine if your list truly ranges from the least anxiety-provoking instances to the most anxiety-provoking instances.

The hierarchy of anxious events should include between ten and fifteen anxious situations in the process of public speaking.[3] If it consists of less than ten, the event has not been broken down enough to use the desensitization process (i.e., the situations will be too intense). If the hierarchy consists of too many events, the technique will take you too long to learn.[4]

You can create your own list of anxious events in public speaking, however, many people who experience anxiety about public speaking report a similar hierarchy of anxious events. Consequently, lists of anxious events that have worked well to help others overcome public speaking anxiety are available.[5] Exercise 8.1 includes such a list of anxious events to guide you in creating your own list.

The communication research on the SD technique shows that your list does NOT have to be an exact hierarchy of anxious situations in order for the technique to be used successfully.[6] What is important is that you have a practical hierarchy to work from that systematically breaks down your event into ten to fifteen situations of smaller anxious events. If the sample list presented in Exercise 8.1 includes most of your anxious situations, you can use this list or rearrange it. If you have other anxious situations in the speechmaking process, you can add them to the sample list and develop your own extended hierarchy of anxious events. Please follow the directions in Exercise 8.1 Parts One and Two.

Exercise 8.2A: Checklist of Anxious Events in Public Speaking

Name   **Date**

To help you create and think about creating your hierarchy of anxious events, please check (√) each event on this list that stimulates any anxiety, fear, or nervousness about public speaking.

1. Thinking about giving your speech while sitting in your room alone

2. Sitting in a room where you are assigned to give a speech

3. Reading a book about how to plan and deliver a speech

4. Hearing about a formal speaking request or assignment

5. Writing your speech or presentation outline

6. Rehearsing your speech alone in a room

7. Rehearsing your speech in front of a few people, friends or family

8. Getting dressed the morning of your presentation

9. Walking to the room and entering it on the day of your speech

10. Waiting to give your speech, while another person speaks or introduces you

11. Walking up to the front of your audience

12. Presenting your speech before the audience and seeing faces look at you

13. Fielding questions after your speech

14. Walking back to your seat after delivering your speech

Exercise 8.2B: Your Hierarchy of Public Speaking Events

Name   **Date**

Now you can create your own hierarchy by identifying specific situations during the speechmaking process that arouse your nervousness and anxiety. In the space provided, record at least ten anxious situations in public speaking. Go back and look at the Hierarchy of Anxious Events in Public Speaking, Part One (you can use any or all items from the list). After listing your situations, rank each instance on a 100-point scale from 1 (least anxiety- producing event) to 100 (most anxiety-producing event) in order to determine the order in your hierarchy (e.g., 20 points=> Reading a textbook about the speechmaking process; 50 points=>Hearing about a formal speaking assignment; 100 points=Presenting a speech before an audience).

Rank Points (1 To 100)	Anxious Instances In Speech Making
1.	
2. e.g., 20	Reading a public speaking book
3.	
4.	
5.	
6.	
7.	
8.	
9.	
10.	
11.	
12.	
13.	
14.	

(TEAR-OUT PAGE FOR PRACTICE AND STUDY)

8.3 Train Your Body in Progressive Muscle Relaxation

For an mp3 download, see: **www.iconquerspeechanxiety.com**

The second step is the heart of the SD technique. It involves training your body to completely relax using prerecorded deep muscle relaxation instructions. SD will be effective for you only if you take time to learn deep muscle relaxation and practice it before moving on to the third step. It is essential that your body learns to differentiate between relaxation and tension, and can maintain the deep relaxation.

SD is NOT hypnosis. It will not bring on a dreamlike state. You will be conscious and in control at all times. Even if you get sleepy, try to stay awake. However, if you fall asleep the first time, don't give up; keep trying to stay awake while you train your body to relax. Busy and stressed people often fall asleep the first time they try to teach their bodies to relax because they have deprived themselves of relaxation and sleep in the rigors of a stressful life. In order to avoid falling asleep, try to practice the relaxation step when you are not overly exhausted and while sitting up in a chair. WARNING: If you lie down in a horizontal position, you will probably doze off and not be able to train your body.

The SD technique uses progressive muscle[7] relaxation training to teach your body to relax. Progressive muscle relaxation involves systematically tensing and holding muscle groups for about five to ten seconds, and then relaxing them for another ten seconds while mentally focusing on how good relaxation feels.[8] Usually each muscle group is tensed and relaxed at least twice before moving on to the next set of muscles. The following muscle groups are successively tensed and then relaxed:

1. Hands (clench)

2. Biceps (bend hands upward at wrist, pointing fingers, flex biceps)

3. Shoulders (shrug shoulders)

4. Neck (push head against chair, then forward)

5. Mouth (press lips tightly)

6. Tongue (extend, retract)

7. Tongue (press to roof and floor of mouth)

8. Eyes and forehead (close eyes tightly, wrinkle forehead)

9. Breathing (inhale, hold, exhale)

10. Back (arch)

11. Midsection (tighten muscles including buttocks)

12. Thighs (tighten muscles)

13. Stomach (suck in stomach)

14. Calves and feet (stretch out both legs)

15. Toes (point toes upward and downward)

The easiest way to train your body in progressive muscle relaxation and the systematic desensitization technique is to use a voice recording. You can use the MP3 file, *iConquer Speech Anxiety: Systematic Desensitization* that is designed to accompany this book (see www.iconquerspeechanxiety.com) or you can create your own recording by using the Systematic Desensitization Script presented in Appendix 1.

You should practice deep muscle relaxation with the recording at least a twice, so your body is trained to know what it means to fully relax, before you move to the third step of SD on the recording.

To prepare to learn deep muscle relaxation, you must take your recording to a quiet room free of distractions and the presence of other people. Do not try to practice SD while driving a car as deep relaxation will interfere with driving and may cause an accident.

You will want to sit upright in a chair, with both feet on the floor. You may want to support your head on a headrest or lean it against a wall. Do not lie down. Remove your glasses, if you like. Allow your arms to rest comfortably on your thighs or the arms of a chair. Play your audio recording of progressive deep muscle relaxation exercises and start learning to relax.

You should practice with your recording until your body is very familiar with relaxation. You want your body to be able to relax on demand, so it will take at least two or even three practice sessions to train your body to bring your muscles to a feeling of deep relaxation.

8.4 Condition Relaxation by Adding Mental Pictures

The third step in the SD technique is to condition your body to relax in response to each and all of the events listed on your hierarchy. To condition relaxation in your body, you will create mental pictures (visualizations) of each of the anxiety-evoking situations listed on your hierarchy of events and at the same time maintain deep muscle relaxation. In other words, you will create a new stimulus-response bond (public speaking with relaxation) as you systematically practice relaxation in response to each of the stimulus situations you bring to mind from your list. The new stimulus-response bond (public speaking <–> relaxation) will replace the old stimulus-response bond (public speaking <–>nervousness/anxiety/physical sensations). For this step, follow the explanation in this chapter and then continue to use the iConquer Speech Anxiety voice recording.

Reciprocal Inhibition or Habituation Explains Conditioning

You may wonder how mentally picturing or visualizing an event while relaxing can condition your body to respond with relaxation at another time in a real situation of public speaking. One explanation is that your body only knows what is happening by what your mind is thinking. If you are completely relaxed when your mind visualizes public speaking, your body has no other way of getting information to the contrary and signals your mind that you are relaxed. Consequently, your body is tricked into learning a relaxation response to the situation you have imagined. The relaxation will be superimposed over your anxiety response, which in turn will weaken. This principle (of superimposing relaxation over anxiety) is called "**reciprocal inhibition**."[9]

Another explanation of how or why SD works is called **"habituation."**[10] Habituation means that as you repeatedly practice a new response to a stimulus, the former response decreases in effect. Therefore, the more you practice SD and visualize the anxiety-provoking situations, the more the old response of nervousness or anxiety weakens and will decrease or go away. You will have conditioned yourself away from the nervousness.

To practice the third step of SD, you must be completely relaxed. You should practice progressive muscle relaxation until every muscle in your body is relaxed. At the point of deep relaxation after you have listened to the recording, begin to add the first four mental pictures from your hierarchy of anxious events. Start first by recalling a neutral or non-anxiety provoking situation in order to practice visualizing a scene. For example, visualize yourself lying in bed just before falling asleep. Try to mentally picture the details in your bedroom with you in the bed feeling completely relaxed.

Once you are relaxed and have practiced visualizing yourself in an anxiety-neutral situation, you are ready to add the first four mental pictures from your hierarchy of anxious events.

Your first set of four mental pictures might include:

1. Thinking about the speech you will give while sitting in your room alone (hold 15 seconds)

2. Sitting in the room where you are being asked to give a speech (hold 15 seconds)

3. Reading a book about planning and delivering a speech (hold 15 seconds)

4. Receiving a formal speaking request or assignment (hold 15 seconds)

You should try to hold the mental picture of each situation for at least fifteen seconds while maintaining complete relaxation. If any muscle becomes tense, clear your mind of the mental picture and concentrate on relaxing that muscle. When all muscles are relaxed, try again to hold the mental picture and maintain complete relaxation for at least fifteen seconds. Do not move on to visualizing the next situation until you can maintain complete relaxation with the previous situation on your hierarchy.

Once you have visualized all of the four lowest anxiety provoking situations from your hierarchy of events, take a few deep breaths, open your eyes, and become acquainted with your surroundings again and stop practice. You should practice with only four new mental pictures at a time in order to give your mind and body a chance to bond relaxation with the mental pictures.

For the next SD practice session, listen to the relaxation recording. Check to see if you can maintain relaxation with the first four mental pictures. If you can, move on to visualizing each of the next four situations from your hierarchy of anxious events.

Your second set of mental pictures might include:

5. Preparing your speech by writing your speech outline

6. Rehearsing your speech alone in your room

7. Rising and getting dressed on the day of the speech

8. Walking to the room and entering it on the day of your speech

Again, when you can maintain complete relaxation for at least fifteen seconds with each situation, take a few deep breaths, open your eyes, and become acquainted with your surroundings.

At your next session, you will again listen to the relaxation part of the recording. Check to see if you can maintain relaxation with the previous four mental pictures. If you can, move on to visualizing each of the final four situations from your hierarchy of anxious events.

Your final set of mental pictures might include:

9. Waiting to give your speech while another person introduces you or speaks

10. Walking up before your audience

11. Presenting your speech before the audience and seeing the faces looking at you

12. Fielding questions after your speech and then walking back to your seat filled with energy and confidence

Plan on Six Practice Sessions

The situation "presenting your speech before the audience" may take some practice before you can hold the visualization and maintain relaxation for at least fifteen seconds. Don't become concerned if you can't hold the visualization and maintain relaxation at first. It will take practice to create the new response bond with the final events listed on your hierarchy. Remember, when you feel tension in a muscle, clear your mind of that mental picture and concentrate on relaxing the muscle. Then when you are relaxed again, return to the mental picture.

You should try to practice the SD exercise, maintaining deep muscle relaxation while going through all three sets of mental pictures several times. You will notice full benefits after you have practiced SD at least six times. It is important that you maintain deep muscle relaxation for each of the mental pictures of your hierarchy in order to form the new relaxation bond to public speaking. Don't move on to the next set of mental pictures until after you have maintained deep muscle relaxation with each mental picture in the previous set. When you have maintained relaxation with every event on your hierarchy, try presenting a short speech to a group of people. As you set small goals for yourself, and practice speaking in public, you may discover new anxiety-provoking situations you want to overcome and can add to your hierarchy list.

If you faithfully practice these three steps in SD, you will notice that your excessive physical sensations (activation) and feelings of nervousness associated with public speaking will diminish over the next few weeks:

1. Create a hierarchy of anxious events or steps in public speaking that are arranged in order of intensity.

2. Train your body in progressive and deep muscle relaxation until your body knows how to completely relax and can differentiate between relaxation and tension.

3. Condition your body to relax in response to all the events on your hierarchy. Visualize only four events at a session so that your body has a chance to create the new stimulus-response bond with each event.

Keep practicing SD and you will acquire new relaxed feelings associated with public speaking.

> **Gina, trainer and human resources specialist,** age 35, wrote: "I used to feel physically out of control when giving a presentation. My body felt like it shook on the inside and outside. Even my voice would shake. My stomach would be in knots. I didn't believe anything could help. But SD did. I practiced SD five or six times…I noticed a big difference by my next presentation. My body felt under control…When I felt comfortable with giving presentations, I was able to apply for a promotion at work and get in training…SD worked for me and I know it will help anyone who faithfully uses it."

Journaling #8 Activity: Learning a New Relaxation Response

Name   **Date**

Today in your journal, reflect on your practice sessions with SD and record how SD is impacting your anxiety level. Use the following points to guide your journaling.

1. Reflect on your experience of learning progressive deep muscle relaxation. How long did you practice it before you could relax? How did you feel when you were completely relaxed? Did you fall asleep at first?

2. Which visualizations from your hierarchy of events were the most difficult to maintain while relaxing? Describe your experience in trying to maintain relaxation while visualizing the situation where you are "presenting your speech before the audience and seeing the faces looking at you."

3. Were you able to practice SD at least three times after you learned progressive muscle relaxation? Explain how you will fit SD into your time schedule and personal plan for conquering speech anxiety (designed in Chapter 5, Exercise 5.5).

4. Describe your public speaking anxiety level now after practicing SD.

Chapter Summary

Systematic desensitization (SD) targets your affect, sensation, and imagery personality dimensions. It is based on learning theory. In the past you unknowingly trained yourself to associate an anxiety response (nervousness and excessive physical activation) with the stimulus (public speaking). In order to break your old stimulus-response bond, you can train your body to associate relaxation with public speaking, forming a new public speaking<–>calm response bond. SD is based on the principles of reciprocal inhibition and habituation. SD involves creating a hierarchy of anxious events or instances in public speaking, training the body in progressive muscle relaxation, and visualizing each of the events in the hierarchy while maintaining deep muscle relaxation. When you have maintained relaxation while visualizing all the events listed on your hierarchy, your excessive physical sensations and feelings of nervous activation associated with public speaking will noticeably diminish.

Review Questions

After reading this chapter, you should be able to answer the following:

1. Which personality dimensions does systematic desensitization (SD) target?

2. What is the goal of SD?

3. Briefly explain the three steps in SD.

4. Describe how to create a hierarchy of anxious events.

5. What is progressive muscle relaxation?

6. How can you train your body in deep muscle relaxation?

7. Contrast the principles of reciprocal inhibition and habituation. Explain how each relates to using SD for overcoming speech anxiety.

8. How many anxious events should you visualize at each practice session? Why?

9. How often should you practice SD before you notice results?

10. What results can be attained from practicing SD?

11. How has SD impacted your public speaking anxiety level?

Notes

[1]Wolpe, 1958

[2]McCroskey, Ralph, & Barrick, 1970; Lane, Cunconan, Friedrich, 2009;

[3]Friedrich, Goss, Cunconan, & Lane, 1997

[4]Butterfield & Booth-Butterfield, 1993, 2001

[5]Friedrich, Goss, Cunconan, & Lane, 1997; Lane, Cunconan, Friedrich, 2009; McCroskey, 1972; Paul, 1966

[6]Yates, 1975

[7]Jacobson, 1938

[8]Friedrich & Goss, 1984

[9]Wolpe, 1958; Friedrich & Goss, 1984

[10]Watts, 1979

CHAPTER NINE
Mental Rehearsal

Mental rehearsal, also called "visualization," is a "cognitive modification" technique. It targets your imagery and cognitive personality dimensions. This technique involves mentally rehearsing an event before participating in it. Many successful athletes have used it to help them attain peak performance. Mental rehearsal helps you visualize success, prepares your mind for the event and thus, helps alleviate some of the situational causes of anxiety. In speechmaking, this technique is practiced just before you give a speech and with a particular speech in mind.

9.1 The Cognitive Psychology of Positive Mental Imagery

According to cognitive psychologists, mental rehearsal is based on the premise that we hold images in our mind of what we perceive as future situations. If the image is negative, then we will feel anxiety.[1] On the other hand, if the image of future situations is positive, then we will have positive feelings and our anxiety will be limited. Consequently, one way to counter feelings of anxiety is to learn to associate positive images or success with a future event, such as public speaking. Mental rehearsal fosters the development of positive thinking and positive images. It will increase your concentration and help you think positively about an upcoming speech. It can help you feel confident and positive instead of negative and anxious.

9.2 Mental Imagery and Athletic Success

The mental rehearsal technique was first developed by Roberto Assagioli[2] in the 1970s and has been used extensively by athletes and trainers since that time.[3] You have probably watched the Olympics in which skiers, gymnasts, runners, and skaters were seated with eyes closed, methodically moving their bodies from side to side to imitate the race in their minds. Many athletes are trained to mentally picture themselves running, skating, skiing, wrestling, or performing their event confidently and successfully before the competition begins.

Mental imagery or mental rehearsal complements behavioral practice (i.e., practicing your speech aloud). Athletes rely on mental rehearsal as a final preparation before the race is run or the game is played, but it cannot and should not ever replace training or practice. It will prepare your mind for a positive and successful experience.

Several athletic studies involving sports from soccer to rugby to tennis to basketball to dart throwing to all types of Olympic competitions have shown the benefit of adding mental imagery to regular skills practice. [4] Studies especially focusing on basketball players, in an effort to improve free-throw shooting, have reported that the practice of mental imagery before games to accompany regular skills practice throughout the week significantly increased the number of free throws made in a game.[5] Again, this research has emphasized that over time the team and individuals, who practiced the combination of mental rehearsal and behavioral rehearsal together found the greatest benefit and enhanced performance.

9.3 Mental Rehearsal and Speech Anxiety

In the mid-1980s, college professors Joe Ayres and Tim Hopf began to use mental imagery, calling the technique "visualization," to help university students decrease their anxiety levels in public speaking classes.[6] Several studies have shown that the technique is very helpful at reducing anxiety when individuals mentally rehearse a very positive and successful speaking experience prior to giving a graded speech in class.[7]

The easiest way to learn mental rehearsal is to practice the technique using a recording designed to help you see yourself in a positive light while giving a speech. You can use the MP3 file, *iConquer Speech Anxiety #4: Mental Rehearsal,* designed to accompany this book www.iconquerspeechanxiety.com or see Appendix 2 for information on creating your own recording using the Mental Rehearsal Script.

It will take about 10 minutes per practice session. When you are ready to practice with the recording, go to a quiet room where you will not be disturbed. Do not try to practice mental rehearsal while driving a car.

To begin a mental rehearsal session, sit upright in a chair and try to become as comfortable as possible. Position your hands on your lap or on the arms of the chair so they feel relaxed. Close your eyes and take three deep diaphragmatic breaths so that your abdomen rises, not your chest. Hold each breath for a few seconds and then slowly release it. Return to your normal breathing pattern. See yourself as the speaker preparing and delivering a specific speech and mentally picture those scenes.

Exercise 9:3: Mental Rehearsal Scenes Practice

In order to practice mental rehearsal, you will need to mentally rehearse scenes like these. So start by having a speech in mind and then try to picture yourself in each of the following scenes.

1. Getting out of bed on the day you will give a speech. You feel energized and confident, and say to yourself, "I am prepared to meet the challenges of the day."

2. Dressing in the clothes that are right for the day and noting your positive attitude

3. Engaging in the activities you usually do before you leave for your presentation

4. Driving and/or walking to the room where you will deliver the speech; practicing diaphragmatic breathing and reciting your positive coping statements as you go

5. Walking into a room filled with warm and friendly people who greet you

6. Taking your seat in the room, conversing very comfortably with others, and feeling confident

7. Waiting for your turn to give the speech while repeating your positive coping statements

8. Moving to the front of the room, feeling very positive about your presentation

9. Delivering your presentation to the audience who is giving you positive feedback with head nods, eye contact, and smiles

10. Introducing your topic with an attention-getter, establishing your credibility, and previewing your points

11. Presenting each main point with evidence--examples, statistics, and quotations

12. Speaking passionately and conversationally, with movement and gesturing

13. Concluding your speech, summarizing main points, and using a memorable ending

14. Receiving applause and praise from your audience

15. Fielding questions confidently

16. Returning to your seat feeling energy and gratification

After you finish visualizing those scenes, return your thoughts to reality, take three diaphragmatic breaths, and then open your eyes.

9.4 Mental Rehearsal on the Day of Your Speech

For an mp3 download, see: **www.iconquerspeechanxiety.com**

Mental rehearsal works best when you practice it close to the time you will be giving your speech. You will want to especially practice this technique the evening before, and the day of your speech. After you have practiced mental rehearsal with the recording, you will be able to re-create the mental imagery without using the recording. This makes the technique very handy to use during a busy day when you can find just a few minutes to sit back and visualize your presentation.

On the day you will be giving a speech, especially try to think only positive thoughts about your speech. Try to visualize the people in your audience with a very positive attitude toward you. Mentally rehearse each part of the speech. Include all of your main points, as well as the introduction and conclusion.

Sam, store manager, age 39, said, "I used to picture myself saying something stupid when speaking in front of any group. I could see everyone laughing at me …I learned a visualization technique as part of a sports program in high school, but I never thought of using something similar for public speaking…Mentally picturing myself doing a good job giving a speech has helped me feel more confident and at ease. I feel more prepared…I will always use visualization to prepare for a presentation."

9.5 Mental Rehearsal & Behavioral Practice Go Together

Mental rehearsal is very important, but it should never take the place of the thorough preparation essential for giving a successful speech. Mental rehearsal works best when it is used along with behaviorally rehearsing your speech. (Remember the basketball teams that mentally and behaviorally rehearsed free throws were the most successful.) Researching your topic, carefully outlining your speech, and thoroughly practicing your delivery will make you feel more comfortable and increase your confidence level.

Behavioral practice means you practice your delivery with an outline on note cards several times before you deliver your speech. It involves practicing your speech aloud, possibly before a mirror, and even practicing it before a few supportive friends or family members. Many people report that the amount of time they spend planning an outline and practicing their delivery has a direct relationship with the security and confidence they feel when they deliver the speech.

If you plan and behaviorally practice your speech, and then practice the mental rehearsal technique to visually rehearse a positive presentation, you will make a giant step toward becoming a confident speaker. You will be able to manage your nervousness and anxiety.

Journaling #9 Activity: Mental & Behavioral Practice

Name   **Date**

Today in your journal, reflect on your mental rehearsal practice sessions and discuss how visualizing positive public speaking experiences is impacting your anxiety level. Use the following points to guide your journaling.

Reflect on a situation where mentally rehearsing your conversation before an important interview or communication encounter helped prepare you for the situation and increase your success. Describe how this technique helped you.

1. If you participated in an athletic event in which visualizing your success was helpful, discuss how you learned visualization and how you used it before a competition.

2. Write a short and realistic script of a few paragraphs on how you will visualize yourself on the day you will give a speech. Include the positive details of the day and your speech.

3. What obstacles have kept you from practicing mental rehearsal more often? Describe what you can do to overcome those obstacles.

4. Discuss the impact that mental rehearsal is having on your public speaking anxiety level now.

Chapter Summary

Mental rehearsal targets the imagery and cognitive personality dimensions. It is based on the premise that we all mentally hold images about future situations. If the image is positive, we have positive feelings; if the image is negative, we feel anxiety. Mental rehearsal stresses the development of positive thinking and positive images. The technique has been used extensively by athletes to attain peak performance and by public speakers to reduce anxiety. At first, you should use a recording to rehearse a positive and successful speaking experience. Later, you can develop your own visualizations of a particular public speaking event. Mental rehearsal works best when you practice it right before you give a speech and with a particular speech in mind. It should never take the place of thorough preparation and behavioral practice. It was designed to complement behavioral rehearsal and prepare your mind for a positive experience.

Review

After reading this chapter, you should be able to answer the following:

1. What personality dimensions does mental rehearsal target?

2. What premise from cognitive psychology is the basis for mental rehearsal?

3. Explain why mental rehearsal should never replace preparation and behavioral practice.

4. Describe how to practice mental rehearsal.

5. When is the best time to practice mental rehearsal?

6. How does behavioral practice complement mental rehearsal.

7. Describe how you have mentally rehearsed an event in your life that helped you become more confident or at ease.

Notes

[1]Fanning, 1988

[2]Assagioli, 1973

[3]Assagioli, 1976; Anthony, Maddox, & Wheatley, 1988;

[4]Clark, 1960; Evans, Jones, & Mullen, 2004; Garfield, 1984, Jordet, 2005; Post, Wrisberg, Mullins 2010; Vealey & Greenleaf, 2010; Kendall, Hrycaiko, Martin, & Kendall, 1990; Driskell, Cooper, Aiden, 1994

[5]Post, Wrisberg, Mullins 2010, Driskell, Cooper, Aiden, 1994; Vassilopoulous, 2005

[6]Ayers & Hopf, 1989

[7]Ayres & Hopf, 1985, 1989; Hopf & Ayres, 1992; Hopf & Ayres, 1992

CHAPTER TEN
Physical Exercise & Interpersonal Support

Physical exercise and interpersonal support help reduce the tension in our lives and thus, target the stress personality dimension. Physical exercise is a research-verified way to reduce stress or anxiety in general, and it has helped public speakers reduce anxiety directly before the presentation. Interpersonal support has been shown to help buffer the impact stress has on our lives. When someone supports us, it often helps us stay committed to our goals, especially challenging goals like overcoming speech anxiety.

10.1 Physical Exercise, Stress & Public Speaking Anxiety

Physical exercise has been shown to benefit a person physiologically, emotionally, cognitively, and even socially.[1] Researchers have found significant improvement in the anxiety, nervousness, and stress levels of people who start exercise programs.[2] Exercisers are better able to manage stress than non-exercisers.[3] In fact, psychologists report, "Vigorous exercise is the natural outlet for the body when it is in the 'fight-flight' state of arousal."[4]

Some physiology researchers have particularly tested the influence of physical exercise on the stress related to public speaking by assessing its impact on a person who exercises directly before delivering a speech.[5] For example, just ten minutes of vigorous bicycle pedaling prior to delivering a speech had a positive effect on the speakers.[6] They reported fewer physiological sensations (e.g., sweating, trembling, nervous stomach, tightness, lumps in the throat, and rapid heart beating), fewer disfluencies (e.g., "uhs," "uhms"), and fewer negative moods, than the speakers who did not exercise before speaking.

One study found significant relationships between the frequency, intensity, and duration of an exercise program and communication anxiety.[6] People who exercised often, with intensity (days worked out to a point of perspiration or breathlessness), and for a longer period of time reported less anxiety or nervousness about giving a speech. In the study, the average workout frequency was 3.5 days per week; the average intensity level (times per week of workout to perspiration or breathlessness) was 2.7 days; and the average duration of a workout was about 49 minutes.[7] In the same study, increased workout intensity was related to decreased anxiety in group discussion, meetings, and overall communication anxiety; increased duration was related to decreased meeting anxiety and overall communication anxiety; increased frequency was related to decreased anxiety in meetings and overall communication anxiety.

Because moderate exercise prior to giving a speech, as well as a general exercise program, helps reduce the reported anxiety and stress levels for those giving a speech, you will want to include exercise in your speech anxiety reduction plan. The Surgeon Generals (present and past) and the U.S. Department of Health and Human Services, as well as most medical and health organizations, recommend a regular exercise program to maintain optimal health.[9]

The author of this book does not advocate a particular exercise program as treatment for public speaking anxiety, but does present this information on exercise and its impact on anxiety for your consideration. You should always consult your physician before starting any exercise program. The point is this: exercise can be helpful in reducing stress and anxiety prior to giving a speech. Consequently, if you have to park a long ways from your work or school and have to face a ten, twenty, or even 30-minute brisk walk every day, consider it therapeutic, especially on the days you will be giving a speech or making a presentation.

Many athletes have an exercise routine they do before a big game or event. The exercise serves to warm up the muscles but also helps reduce pre-game nervousness or anxiety. No one seems to discuss how funny those football players look doing exercises on the field before kickoff. We all know they are doing warm-up exercises. In the same way, public speakers need warm-up routines to reduce anxiety and get the blood flowing into the limbs. They should not be ashamed to "warm up" for a speech by doing anxiety-reducing exercises.

The Windmill Warm-Up exercise combines the deep abdominal breathing technique from Chapter Six with arm movements for physical exercise. It is one exercise that individuals have used as part of their warm-up routines prior to delivering presentations. Try practicing the Windmill Warm-Up in Exercise 10.3 before you give a presentation.

Exercise 10.1: Windmill Warm-Up Exercise

The Windmill Warm-Up combines physical activity with deep abdominal breathing. Just like athletes who exercise before a game to warm up and relieve stress, you too can use physical exercise and deep breathing to relieve stress before a speech. Follow these steps:

1. Stand up straight, with shoulders thrown back and head reaching to the ceiling. (Move your arms forward and back around your head slowly to make sure you have enough room to practice this exercise without hitting someone.)

2. Place your arms out in front of you.

3. Inhale deeply and hold your breath.

4. Now, swing both arms backward in a circle two times and then swing them forward in a circle two times.

5. Stop and exhale slowly and fully until all of your air is exhaled.

6. Then, tell your body to go limp and to RELAX.

Repeat the Windmill Warm-Up exercise several times, especially when you have been sitting at a desk or riding in a car for a long time. It will help reduce tension before delivering a speech, warm up your muscles, and get the blood flowing to your fingertips (to reduce cold hands, generated by the fight-flight-freeze response).

Figure 10.1 The Windmill

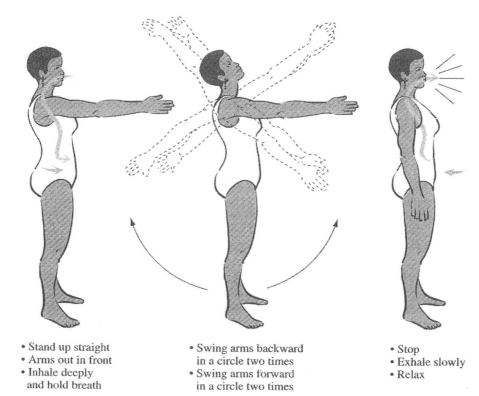

• Stand up straight
• Arms out in front
• Inhale deeply
  and hold breath

• Swing arms backward
  in a circle two times
• Swing arms forward
  in a circle two times

• Stop
• Exhale slowly
• Relax

10.2 Interpersonal Support Reduces Stress

Interpersonal support, also called social support or mutual support, means we have others in our lives who share similar struggles, similar emotions, and similar ideas.[10] Several studies have reported that social support, by enhancing feelings of commonality and belongingness, helps us manage stress in general, buffers its impact on our lives, and helps us stay committed to our goals.[11]

Weight reduction groups, such as Weight Watchers, for decades have been very successful at helping people lose weight or maintain it though social support and accountability. Exercise programs, such as Curves or Jazzercise, have helped many people adhere to work outs by providing social support while doing exercise routines. Recovery groups, such as Alcoholics Anonymous or Gamblers Anonymous, have given mutual support to many in their efforts to overcome addictions. In the same way, you can be helped by social support in your efforts to overcome speech anxiety.

Social support for conquering speech anxiety is best discovered in a group where people are working toward the same goals and can be mutually supportive of one another. A public speaking class or workshop designed for those with anxiety about public speaking is a good place to find people who have the same goals as you have. Such classes can help you feel that you are not alone in your attempt to become a confident speaker. In addition, they will provide you with a supportive environment, special help, and a safe arena to practice public speaking skills.[12] Many individuals have reported that the encouragement they received from others in a public speaking class is what built their confidence and enabled them to learn more skills. In fact, recent studies on public speaking anxiety have shown that repeated practice of speeches in a very supportive environment and in front of the same audience has helped individuals significantly reduce speech anxiety.[13]

If you do not have the support of a special class or club, then you should try to find supportive friends to share your progress, but do not share your struggle to conquer speech anxiety with judgmental friends who have no interest in public speaking. You cannot expect them to be supportive when you practice a speech or discuss a new technique or share your progress.

Journaling #10 Activity: Plan for Physical Exercise and Social Support

Name   **Date**

Today in your journal, you will reflect on your physical exercise plan and the interpersonal support in your life that can aid in reducing public speaking anxiety. Use the following points to guide your journaling.

1. Reflect on the stressors (things that cause stress) in your life. Discuss if and how you are getting enough physical exercise, sleep, and other health measures to combat the stressors in your life.

2. If you are not getting enough exercise to help reduce stress in your life, describe where you can go to get help.

3. Discuss your plan to develop a healthy stress-reduction program in your life.

4. Write about your plan to increase social support in your life, especially for conquering your public speaking anxiety.

Chapter Summary

Physical exercise targets the stress personality dimension because it helps reduce stress and anxiety in general. It has been shown to be most helpful for reducing communication anxiety when a person exercises often (about 3.5 times per week), with intensity (working to a point of perspiration), for a longer period of time (about fifty minutes). Physical exercise specifically reduces anxiety for public speakers when practiced directly before a presentation. You may find that even a brisk walk will help reduce anxiety before delivering a speech. Social support also targets the stress personality dimension because it helps reduce stress in general and buffers its impact on your life. Social support helps you stay committed to your goals and experience a sense of commonality and belongingness that is important when developing any new skill or overcoming any challenge. Enrolling in a basic public speaking class or workshop where you can find the support from others who have the same public speaking goals and anxieties can help you reduce your anxiety and gain confidence.

Review Questions

After reading this chapter, you should be able to answer the following:

1. What personality dimension does physical exercise target?

2. Explain how physical exercise helps reduce speech anxiety.

3. What personality dimension does interpersonal support target?

4. Explain how interpersonal support can help a person overcome speech anxiety.

5. Where can you expect to find interpersonal support for overcoming speech anxiety?

6. Describe your plan to increase interpersonal support in your life for overcoming speech anxiety.

Notes

[1]Sachs, 1982

[2]Otto, 1990; Sachs, 1982; Sedlock & Duda, 1994

[3]Stone, 1987

[4]Davis, Eshelman, & McKay, 2008; Eshelman, McKay, & Fanning p. 225

[5]Otto, 1990; Schwartz & Kaloupek, 1987; Sedlock & Duda, 1994

[6]Otto, 1990

[7]Thomas, Dwyer, & Rose, 2001

[8]Thomas, et al., 2001

[9] U.S. Department of Health and Human Services, 1996, 2010

[10]Jacobs, Masson, Harvill, & Schimmel, 2012

[11]Lakey, B., 2010; Daniels & Guppy, 1994; Overholser, Norman, & Miller, 1990; Ray & Miller, 1994

[12]Dwyer, 1998; Dwyer & Cruz, 1998; Dwyer & Fus, 1999, 2002; Dwyer, Carlson, & Kahre, 2002

[13]Finn, Sawyer, & Schrodt, 2009

CHAPTER ELEVEN
Skills Training

Skills Training targets the behavior personality dimension. It is essential for developing confidence and competence in public speaking. Learning what to do in public speaking situations will help reduce situational anxiety caused by a perceived lack of skills and the novelty or ambiguity of not knowing what is necessary for an effective presentation.

11.1 Skills Training Builds Skills and Reduces Anxiety

Because anyone can become anxious about doing something new when they do not know how to do it, skills training (also called rhetoritherapy) is designed to help people learn and improve specific public speaking behaviors.1 In learning and practicing the skills for effective public speaking, the ambiguity of the situation is diminished and anxiety is greatly reduced.[2]

The skills training technique relies on the skills deficit model,[3] which assumes people avoid communication because of perceived lack of skills and novelty of the situation. A perceived lack of skills triggers anxiety in communication situations, which in turn leads to further avoidance and increased fear. In other words, the more you believe you lack the skills, the more anxiety you experience, more you will avoid public speaking where you could learn and practice the skills you need and the more anxious you can become. In order to break the anxiety- avoidance chain, you will want to enroll in a workshop, a public speaking fundamentals class or a public speaking club, where you can learn how to become an effective speaker and practice the skills.

Keep in mind, communication research indicates that skills training works well to reduce anxiety when it is taught in combination with other anxiety-reduction techniques[4] and when other treatment techniques are taught first.[5] Consequently, if you previously tried to learn public speaking skills in a class or other venue, but retreated because of intense anxiety, you probably needed to learn other anxiety-reduction techniques first (e.g., SD, diaphragmatic breathing, cognitive restructuring) before attempting to learn public speaking skills. A dimension other than behavior was most likely at the top of your firing order. Thus, before you join a class or speaking club at this time, you will want to practice SD, diaphragmatic breathing and the cognitive restructuring coping statements. These techniques will further prepare you for success in learning the new skills.

11.2 Skills Training Targets One Behavior at a Time

The skills training technique is most effective because it carefully targets specific behaviors for improvement, such as topic selection, organization, verbal and nonverbal delivery.[7] Thus, you should enroll in a class, workshop or club where you can focus on developing specific skills, one or two at a time.

Effective skills training includes these components:

1. Identifying a skill you need to learn or adjust (a deficiency)

2. Observing models of the skilled behavior

3. Setting attainable goals

4. Acquiring knowledge about the new skill

5. Visualizing the new skill

6. Practicing the new skill in a nonthreatening and natural environment,

7. Self-monitoring your progress.[8]

You will want to look for classes or workshops that are designed especially to help individuals overcome speech anxiety. Begin by asking local college advisors about the availability of such programs. Specialized public speaking classes will teach you specific behaviors through skills training, as well as help you learn the other anxiety-reduction techniques. If a special class designed to help reduce nervousness and anxiety about public speaking is not available, choose a basic public speaking class or workshop that encourages you to set modest and specific goals with each speaking opportunity, or join an organization (e.g., Toastmasters) that encourages beginning speakers on how to develop basic skills. For example, a first assignment or opportunity might include a short one- or two-minute mini-presentation on a familiar topic in which you can practice specific behaviors before moving on to longer speaking opportunities.

11.3 Skills Training Covers Basic Skills

A basic public speaking course will teach you how to introduce, organize, research, and deliver informative, as well as persuasive speeches. Individuals who complete a basic public speaking course report significantly less communication anxiety and more competence than when they started the class.[9]

Some of the specific skills you will learn in a basic public speaking course include:

1. Choosing a topic

2. Selecting a specific purpose and central idea

3. Analyzing the audience and situation

4. Researching the topic and adding supporting material

5. Organizing and outlining the ideas

6. Creating introductions and conclusions

7. Preparing note cards and visual aids

8. Rehearsing and delivering a speech

Because learning public speaking skills is an important step in becoming an effective and confident speaker, now would be a good time to assess your public speaking skills by completing Exercise 11.3.

Exercise 11.3: Public Speaking Skills Assessment

Name   **Date**

Learning public speaking skills is an important step in becoming an effective and confident speaker.

1. Please read though the following list of basic public speaking skills and check (√) the skills you need to learn in order to become a confident and effective speaker.

   a. Choosing your topic

   b. Selecting a specific purpose and central idea for your speech

   c. Analyzing your audience and the situation

   d. Researching the topic and incorporating supporting material into your speech

   e. Organizing and outlining your ideas

   f. Creating introductions and conclusions

   g. Preparing note cards and visual aids

   h. Rehearsing and delivering your speech

2. Now please summarize your skills and those skills you most need to learn to become an effective speaker.

(TEAR-OUT PAGE FOR PRACTICE AND STUDY)

11.4 Basic Skills to Get You Started

Each of the skills in Exercise 11.3: Public Speaking Skills Assessment will be briefly explained in the following paragraphs. These explanations are in no way intended to replace what you can learn in a public speaking course or workshop, but are summaries and tips to help you get started in learning public speaking skills.

Choosing a Topic

Choosing a topic is one of the hardest decisions for new speakers to make. The best advice is threefold: (1) choose a topic on which you have personal experience and knowledge; (2) choose a topic for which you are passionate or enthusiastic; and (3) choose a topic you are willing to research for additional information.

You will find it much easier to prepare a speech and give it if you already know something about the topic and have had experience with it. Consider topics that include your college major, your work, your hobbies, your vacations, or your passions. You can start by brainstorming these categories of topics. Write down anything that comes to mind and then narrow the topic for the goal of the assigned speech and for the audience. For example, while brainstorming, Zach listed his part-time job at a local hardware store where he learned how to install faucets. For his speech, Zach chose to show his audience how they could easily replace a leaky faucet with an inexpensive new one.

Selecting a Specific Purpose and Central Idea

Once you have chosen your topic, you will need to determine your purpose and central idea (also called a thesis statement). Think of your specific purpose and central idea as the destination you hope to reach on your journey of preparing your speech. Like following a road map, they will remind you of the important points of interest and the place where you hope to end your journey.

You will usually start with a general purpose, often assigned to you by a contact person, boss, or instructor. Usually, your general purpose will fall into one of three categories: to inform, to persuade, or to entertain. Once you have your general purpose, you can move to your specific purpose; that is the unique goal for your speech. A specific purpose often begins like this: "To inform (or to persuade) my audience to . . ." It should include the number of aspects, reasons, or steps you hope your audience will remember by the end of your speech. For example, Jan's specific purpose for her informative speech was, "To inform my audience about the four most important skills for winning in volleyball."

The central idea, also called the core idea or thesis statement, is a brief, one-sentence summary of what you will say. It is the gist of your speech. It includes the number of points as stated in your specific purpose, and it briefly mentions each main point. For example, because Jan's specific purpose was "To inform my audience about the four most important skills for winning in volleyball," Jan's central idea was, "The four most important skills winning in volleyball are focused on passing, setting, spiking, and digging." Jan's four main points will cover passing, setting, spiking, and digging. Again, your specific purpose and central idea will guide the development of your speech and keep you focused on your goal.

Analyzing the Audience and Situation

From start to finish, the most important consideration in planning and presenting a speech is your audience. To be an effective speaker, you must be audience-centered. That means you need to assess and consider who your audience is, what their interests are, what their age group or gender is, and what their knowledge and concerns about your topic include. Before going any further with a topic, you will want to make sure that you can make your topic interesting to your audience. For example, if the audience comprises college students, you need to choose a topic that you can make interesting to that age group and educational experience. If your audience comprises people in their late fifties or sixties, you need to keep in mind what would be the history, background, and concerns of that age group.

Your NUMBER ONE consideration should focus on how you will help your audience. As discussed in Chapter Three and Chapter Seven, every audience is looking for helpful or useful ideas to enrich their lives or help them in some way. Secondly, they are hoping the speaker cares about their welfare and is not trying to deceive them with a gimmick or gainful fraud or trickery. Consequently, your goal is to let the audience know from the beginning how your information will help them and that you are concerned for their welfare. For example, Zach reminded his audience members that by learning how to install their own faucet to replace one that leaks, they could fix a common problem they will definitely face sometime and in the process save close to $100 in a plumbing bill.

Researching the Topic and Adding Supporting Material

In order to make your speech interesting to your audience and give it substance, you need to research your topic so that you can include interesting facts, quotations, statistics, and examples in your introduction, main points, and conclusion. When incorporated into your speech, quotations, statistics, and examples are called supporting material.

Examples help your audience understand what you mean. Quotations and statistics help your audience understand why your points are important, why you are credible and why they should believe you.

Examples illustrate a point, describe a situation, clarify meaning, and personalize your ideas. You audience is most likely to remember your examples at the end of your speech, which will help them remember your points. All examples or illustrations should be descriptive, engaging, and help your audience visualize the situation.

In his speech, Zach used an example to describe a situation when one of the handles from a spraying faucet broke off and water gushed out all over a neighbor's kitchen. The neighbor called for a plumber and paid double time in wages for the plumber to come on a Saturday. On top of that, the plumber took over two hours to get to the neighbor's house to fix the kitchen explosion of water. Zach's example engaged his audience and helped them personalize their own need to know how to change a faucet when the situation occurs quickly and unexpectedly.

Expert quotations include testimonies or accounts of the facts by professionals in the field (e.g., doctors, authors, professors, researchers, policemen, etc.). Quotations add expert advice and credibility. Zach added this quotation to his first main point, "In an article by Roger Getz, from Plumbing Today Magazine, June 2011, Getz said: Most homeowners will need to have a faucet replaced sometime in their lifetime and the cost will likely exceed $100." The expert quotation from Plumbing Today Magazine reinforced the importance of learning how to replace your own faucet.

Peer quotations are not authoritative or expert. They are not meant to be, but they add knowledge and emotion to help the listeners relate to the situation. For example, Zach added this quotation from his neighbor, "I just wish I had known what to do to repair the faucet and keep the water from ruining my kitchen floor and downstairs ceiling." Both expert quotations and peer quotations help the audience understand and remember your points.

Statistics are numerical data that show dates, times, trends, and relationships. They strengthen your points. In his speech, Zach added credibility and topic importance when he said, "I spoke to Mr. Brad Peters, who owns Peter's Plumbing, who said, 'Installing a new faucet could run more than $300 on the weekend.'" When Zach quantified the importance of saving money and not having to rely on a plumber for a simple project, his audience seemed eager to learn the faucet installation process.

The best places to search for statistics, examples, and quotations are in reliable print sources--magazines, books, professional journals, newspapers, government documents, or news outlets. Your supporting material should be recent and sponsored by established and impartial news outlets or broadcasting networks. You should not use online sources such as blogs or wikis which have no accountability or peer review for accuracy.

Be sure to keep a record of the sources for all supporting material used as you always need to cite the source by mentioning four elements that help the listeners determine credibility or find it as needed. The four elements include the source, the date, the author, and the author's credibility. For example, for a speech about tsunamis, you might cite your sources by saying:

According to journalist (Credibility) Geoff Tibballs (Author), who wrote Tsunami: The Most Terrifying Disaster book (Source), in 2004 (Date) at least 300,000 people were swept to their deaths as the giant wave devastated everything in its path for over 2000 miles (example of a book citation).

OR

In a Canadian Geographic article entitled Wave Warning (Source) written by geologist (Credibility), Tara Efron, (Author) published in October 2010 (Date): When a tsunami warning is sounded at least one half-hour in advance, most lives have been saved (example of a magazine/journal citation).

All good speeches will include supporting material in the points. In addition, all sources for your supporting material should be listed in the reference list of your outline.

Organizing and Outlining the Ideas.

All speeches should include these three parts:

1. Introduction,

2. Body, and

3. Conclusion.

Because you need to know what your points will be before you can introduce and conclude them, start with organizing the body before you work on the introduction. To quickly begin work on developing main points, consider using a mind map.

Creating a simple mind map is a very effective and easy way to begin to organize your ideas for a presentation. To make a mind map, start with a piece of notebook paper and a pencil. First write the name or topic of your speech at the top and then write down all ideas that come to mind. Brainstorming means you write down as many ideas as possible about your topic over a few minutes of time without being judgmental about the ideas. Use only a few words for each thought. You can go back later to pick the ideas that you think will most helpful and interesting to your audience.

When you start brainstorming, again try to let your ideas flow from your mind to the paper. After you have written out your ideas, choose three to five solid and interesting main points and draw circles around them. See the example in Figure 11.1. Then give each point a short name and number those points in an order you think might make the presentation clear and easy to follow.

In skills training, you will learn helpful organizational patterns for arranging the order of main points, such as chronological, cause-effect, problem-solution, or topical, etc. Now that you have provisionally selected main points, draw lines from your main points to other ideas that relate to each main point. You will be creating subpoints. Next, you can draw double lines from the sub-points to other appropriate ideas, thus, creating sub subpoints. See Figure 11.1 and simple example for Zach's Mind Map for a speech on Installing a New Faucet.

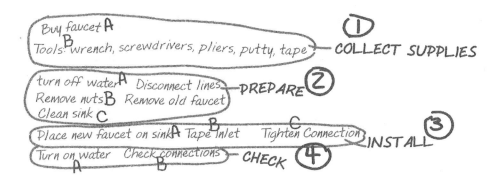

Figure 11. 1

Once you have mapped out your speech main points, sub-points, and sub sub-points, you can create a formal outline, using Roman numerals, capital letters, etc. A formal outline will include a formal format and indentations for the body as well as for the introduction and conclusion. See the following Chart for a basic speech outline template. Place your source citations in parentheses after each point or sub-point in your outline. At the end of your outline, add a reference list with all the sources used in your speech. When you have completed the outline of your body, you are ready to create the introduction and conclusion.

Basic Outline Template for a Speech

Introduction

I. **Interest** (Use an attention-getter): Engage the audience in your topic (e.g., use a story, pertinent humor, startling statistic etc.).

II. **Importance** (Describe significance to your audience): Tell your audience why your topic is important and how it will help them.

III. **Involvement** (Establish your credibility): Explain your expertise or connection to your topic.

IV. **Ingredients** (Preview your main points): Mention briefly the points you will cover in your presentation (e.g., "In this speech you will learn…" or "we will cover.").

Body

I. **Use three to five MAIN POINT S.**
   A. Use at least two SUBPOINTS for each main point.
      1. Add facts in your SUB SUBPOINTS.
      2. Use examples, quotes, and statistics in your sub-subpoints (include sources).
         a. SUB-SUB SUBPOINTS go here
         b. use phrases or descriptive words
   B. Use at least two SUBPOINTS for each main point.
      1. You need to have at least two SUB-SUBPOINTS for each sub-point.
      2. You should NOT have "1" without "2" or "a" without "b."

(**Transition:** Use a bridge to link previous point to the next main point [e.g., "Now we have discussed the problem, let's turn to the solution"]).

II. **You will need two or more MAIN POINTS.**
   A. Add the SUBPOINTS.
   B. Use the same format shown above in Main Point I.

Conclusion

I. **Signpost** (Signal word): Alert the audience you are ending (e.g., say in conclusion, to summarize, finally).

II. **Summary** (Review points): Summarize your main points succinctly.

III. **Importance** (Recap significance): Remind the audience how the information is important or helpful for them.

IV. **Memorable Ending:** End with a final statement that leaves an impact (e.g., a powerful quotation, a story/ example that relates to the one used in the introduction, a call to action with a declaration that you too are taking action, etc.).

Reference List

Author's Name (Date of Publication). Title of book. Place of Publication:
   Publisher's Name.
Example: Dwyer, K. (2005). Conquer Your Speech Anxiety. New York:
   Wadsworth.

**Author's Name (Date). Title of article. Journal/ Magazine title,
   volume #, page numbers.**
Example: Miller, K. (2011). Taming speech fright. Lifetime Magazine, 6,
   33-38.

Creating Introductions

   Introductions and conclusions are essential parts of any speech. Effective
introductions engage your audience by drawing their interest into your topic.
Memorable conclusions help your audience remember your points and their
importance. The important parts of an effective introduction are easy to
remember using the four "I's": Interest,

Importance, Involvement, and Ingredients

   First, get the audience's interest and attention for your topic. To do this, you
could tell a vivid story, use an expert quotation, refer to a current event, give a
statistic, or share a personal example. Whatever attention getter you choose, it
should be one that introduces your topic and makes it interesting to your
audience. Never tell a story that is unrelated to the topic, or is longer in time
than 10% of your speech, or is in bad taste for the audience members.

   Next, remind the audience how important the topic is for them and how
your topic could be helpful to their lives. This will motivate them to listen by
giving them a reason to stay focused on your message.

   Third, tell the audience about your personal involvement with the topic or
how you know about your subject. Sharing your experience with the topic will
help establish your credibility. When a speaker has high credibility, the audience
is more likely to believe the message.

   Lastly, preview the main ingredients of your speech (main points) so the
audience knows what to expect in your speech. If you introduce your speech

well, so that your audience is interested in your topic and looking forward to hearing the points, you will be off to a very good start. For example, Zach might say, "Today I will help you learn how to replace a leaky faucet in four easy steps: 1) collect your tools, 2) prepare your plumbing area, 3) install the new faucet, and 4) check how it works.

Creating Conclusions

Effective conclusions leave your audience with a lasting impression, as well as help your audience remember your main points and their importance. The important parts of an effective conclusion can be easily remembered by again using four "I's": In conclusion, Ingredients, Importance, and Interest. As you come to the end of your speech, signal your audience that you are concluding by using words such as "in conclusion" or "finally." Then, briefly summarize the main ingredients of your speech so that your audience will have a chance to remember your main points one more time. Next, remind your audience about the importance of the topic or how they can use the information in their lives. Finally, leave your audience with a memorable impression that will interest them and have a positive impact, such as a thought-provoking question, a quotation, a challenge, or humorous story. If you end your speech with an effective conclusion, you will leave your audience with a lasting impression. For example, Zach might retell his neighbor's story with a happy ending and a small bill with much money saved.

Preparing Speaker's Note Cards

Once you have your outline prepared, with an introduction and conclusion, you are ready to make speaker's note cards and create visual aids. Since small index cards (3x5) are hard to read, use larger unlined 5x8 index cards for your note cards and position the cards vertically. Write or type in large print on the cards so that if you leave them on a lectern and step back six feet, you can still read the words. Print only four to five key words per line for each point, sub-point, and sub sub-point. The key words should jog your memory for each point. Place any cited sources for a particular point in parentheses next to the point. When you deliver your speech, try not to hold your cards so they are noticeable to your audience. Instead, leave them on a lectern and touch them only as you need to turn them.

Creating Visual Aids

The purpose of visual aids is to help the audience understand your ideas, remember your points, and stay interested in your speech topic. For you, visual aids can also help reduce speech anxiety by giving you something to do with your hands and by focusing audience attention away from you.6   Visual aids that enhance your message can range from presentational software such as PowerPoint slides, to multimedia software such as Prezi, to models or objects or charts or video. Make sure your visual aids look neat and professional since they represent you as the speaker. They should be simple, but large enough for all to see.

Visual aids should be interesting for your audience. Under no circumstances, should your visual aids include presentational slides that have your entire speech outline written out. Instead, use bulleted words or points with no more than three to four words per line and only three to four lines per slide. Use a 36-point font size for titles, 24-point for subtitles, and no smaller than 18-point for sub-subtitles so that your audience will be able to read your points. In addition, use upper and lower case for the print; do not use all CAPS as capital letters are hard for the audience to read.

When you display objects, hold them up so all in your audience have a clear view. Never pass them around the room; if you do, people will watch the visual aid going around the room and miss what you are saying. Explain your visual aid and make it an integral part of your speech. Make sure you maintain eye contact with your audience so that you do not look like you are talking directly to your visual aid. Lastly, practice your speech with your visual aid so that you are comfortable handling it and can display it while maintaining eye contact with your audience.

Rehearsing and Delivering a Speech

If you want to be an effective speaker, you must rehearse your speech and practice effective delivery techniques before you deliver a speech. Never read your speech unless you are the President of the United States, or hold another office of high authority, where every word you utter is scrutinized by the news media and the rest of the world. You need to practice your delivery so you can speak from note cards with the few key words that prompt your memory. Try to look up at your audience more than you look down at your cards. Read your speech over at least once to yourself. Then practice your speech aloud several times.

In the beginning when you practice your speech, it may sound bumpy and you may forget some things. Don't lose heart. This is part of the rehearsal process. The more times you speak your speech aloud, the more you will learn it, and the more the ideas will come to mind and easily flow out to your audience. Every time you practice, check your timing to make sure you fulfill the time requirements of your presentation. Try to practice with your visual aid so that you can use it effortlessly. If you use presentational software, make sure you practice by looking at the display to check your slides and NOT at your screen.

When you are comfortable practicing your speech aloud with note cards, find a supportive friend or family member to be your audience for a dress rehearsal. You could even practice with thick books stacked on a table to simulate using a lectern. Finally, you may want to record your speech as you practice so you can hear how you sound when speaking to an audience and be able to make adjustment.

As we have discussed in several of the previous chapters, conversational delivery works best for delivering a speech. You can be yourself and use the same conversational style that you use every day with family and friends. However, you will want to make a few adjustments to accommodate your audience. For example, practice speaking loudly enough so that the people in the back of the room can hear you. Practice adding enthusiasm and vocal variation (change in voice projection and tone) so that your audience finds it easy to remain alert as opposed to drifting off to the sounds of a monotonous voice. Ask your dress rehearsal audience to raise a hand if you speak too fast or too softly so you can make slight adjustments in your voice, as needed.

On the Day of Your Presentation

On the day of your presentation, dress in a way that matches your topic and adds credibility to your speech. For example, you might dress in a suit if your topic is professional and related to your career, such preparing an interview or you might wear the shirt with the hardware store logo if your presentation is on installing a new faucet, or you might wear workout clothing if your topic is new moves for a *Zumba* class.

When you walk to the front of the room to deliver your speech, walk as if you have all the confidence in the world. Follow the old adage, "Fake it until you make it." Imagine how a confident person and speaker would walk. Then practice walking the same way. Your level of confidence will grow because your body will adopt the new confident gait. Place your note cards on the lectern and smile at your audience. Remember, your audience is interested in knowing that you care about them. So smile at each of the members as if to say, "I'm glad you're here. We are going to have a good time together today."

SOFTEN Your Delivery

As you speak to your audience, try to use confident nonverbal delivery behaviors that show you care about your audience and your topic. One way to remember the six confident and caring nonverbal delivery behaviors you will display is to follow the acronym SOFTEN.[10]

The acronym **SOFTEN** can help you remember your nonverbal delivery cues. **SOFTEN stands for the following:**

S=Smile

O=Open Posture

F=Forward Lean

T=Touch

E=Eye Contact

N=Nod

SMILE graciously as you walk to the front of the room to speak, when you speak, and when you answer questions. This tells your audience members that you like them and are glad they are there.

Use **OPEN POSTURE** as you stand in front of the audience. Do this by uncrossing your legs and arms and by keeping your arms slightly forward, and bent, and at your sides or resting them on the lectern in front of you.

Use a **FORWARD LEAN** to show interest in your audience. Lean forward and move toward your audience whenever possible. If you lean backwards, you show you are less interested in making a connection with your audience members.

Reach out with your hands as if to **TOUCH** your audience. To add gestures to you delivery, occasionally extend your hands out and wide to your audience as if you were reaching out to touch them in your motions. You will want to refrain from touching your hair, your face, and your jewelry or from rubbing your hands together. Such behaviors distract the audience from listening to you.

Try to establish **EYE CONTACT** with each person at least once. Try to look at the listeners on your left, on your right, and in front of you. If you find it difficult to maintain eye contact at first, try looking for very friendly nonthreatening faces on each side of the room and in the front. This will get you started at looking at all areas of the room. Eye contact signals friendliness, interest, and competence. To be an effective speaker, you do not have to maintain eye contact with audience members 100% of the time. Your goal is to look up from your notes more than you look down.

Occasionally **NOD** and use positive head movements when people ask questions at the end of your presentation. Nodding lets people know that you are listening and understanding their questions or concerns. If someone asks you a question that you can't answer, simply nod and say, "That's a good question; I will research the answer and get back to you."

> **Zach (construction engineer), age 29**, said, "I cannot get over how helpful it was to join Toastmasters and then to enroll in a public speaking class...Once I really practiced deep breathing and SD for a few weeks plus memorized the coping statements, the new skills took away most of my remaining anxiety... I recommend that everyone learns and practices diaphragmatic breathing, SD and the coping statements. Then when you learn the skills...you will be surprised at how much it can improve your anxiety level and confidence."

This section has covered the very basics of public speaking skills that you will learn along with many others when you enroll in a public speaking workshop or course. These skills were offered in an attempt to get you started thinking about effective communication skills. As you acquire public speaking skills in concert with applying the other techniques presented in this book, you will significantly reduce your anxiety and nervousness about public speaking. You will become a confident and effective speaker. Now complete the following journaling activity to help reinforce what you have learned in this chapter.

Journaling #11 Activity: Skills Training
Name   **Date**

   Today in your journal, reflect on your public speaking skills. Discuss the skills you have learned, the skills you need to learn, and how learning public speaking skills can impact your public speaking anxiety level. Use the following points to guide your journaling:

1. Based on the summary of public speaking skills presented in section 11.3, discuss the effective public speaking skills that you have already acquired and how you have acquired them.

2. Discuss the skill descriptions that surprised you the most section in 11.3 and why.

3. Describe the public speaking skills that you need to acquire or enhance in order to become an effective speaker.

4. Are you enrolled in a public speaking course or workshop now? If not, write down the steps you will take to find and then enroll in such a course or even join a public speaking club.

5. Visualize yourself practicing the nonverbal skills of the acronym SOFTEN and then write a description about how you see yourself looking and feeling.

6. Discuss the impact skills training is having on your public speaking anxiety level or what impact you hope it will have on your progress.

Chapter Summary

In summary, skills training targets the behavior personality dimension. Acquiring public speaking skills is essential to developing confidence and effectiveness as a public speaker, as well as reducing speech anxiety from perceived lack of skills. Try to choose a public speaking fundamentals class that encourages you to set modest and specific goals with each speaking opportunity. The basic skills you will learn include: choosing your topic, selecting a specific purpose and central idea for your speech, analyzing your audience and the situation, researching the topic and incorporating supporting material into your speech, organizing and outlining your ideas, creating introductions and conclusions, preparing note cards and visual aids, rehearsing and delivering your speech.

As you acquire public speaking skills while applying the other anxiety-reduction techniques presented in this book, you will significantly reduce nervousness about public speaking. You will become a confident and effective speaker.

Review Questions

After reading this chapter, you should be able to answer the following:

1. Which personality dimension does skills training target?

2. Where can you go to learn the skills training technique?

3. Describe the public speaking skills you need to learn the most.

4. Brainstorm as many topics as possible that you could use for a five-minute informative speech for a college class or speaking club or business group.

5. Choose one topic from your list in #4 above and create a mind map of main points, sub-points and sub sub-points.

6. How will you acquire more public speaking skills in the next few weeks or months?

Notes

[1]Fremouw & Zitter, 1978; Fawcett & Miller, 1975; Kelly, 1997, Kelly & Keaten, 2000, 2009; Kelly, Duran, & Stewart, 1990; Kelly, Phillips, & Keaten, 1995; Phillips, 1977

[2]Whitworth & Cochran, 1996

[3]Phillips, 1991

[4]Allen, Hunter, & Donohue, 1989; Ayres & Hopf, 1993, 1994; Dwyer, 1995; Rossi & Seiler, 1989; Whitworth & Cochran, 1996

[5]Ayers & Hopf, 1993; Ayres, Hopf, Hazel, Sonandre, & Wongprasert, 2009

[6]Ayres, 1991

[7]Richmond & McCroskey, 1998

[8]Glaser, 1981; Kelly, 1989; Richmond & McCroskey, 1998

[9]Rubin, Rubin, & Jordan, 1997

[10]Wassmer, 1990

KAREN KANGAS DWYER

Personal Notes

Part Three: Putting It All Together
CHAPTER TWELVE
You Can Conquer Speech Anxiety

Do you feel inspired? You should! Speech anxiety is not an unconquerable monster. You can do it! But remember, in the same way that passively watching a videotape on aerobic exercise will not improve your physical well-being, so too passively reading this book will not magically make your speech anxiety disappear. To conquer your speech anxiety, you need to put together all that you have learned into a personal plan that you will follow. As Chapter One pointed out, you will want to: (1) Commit yourself to the goal of conquering speech anxiety; (2) Check on your progress at actively learning the techniques targeted to your firing order; (3) Check your practice schedule to ensure you are practicing the techniques regularly; and (4) Participate in public communication so you can put your new knowledge, techniques, and skills to use.

12.1 Commit Yourself to Your Goal

The most important step you can take now is to commit yourself to your goal of conquering speech anxiety. By reading this book you are on your way! Make sure you have done all the exercises. Go back and check each of them NOW. If you have skipped any of the exercises, DO THEM. Read over your answers to Exercises 1.3 and 2.4. Reaffirm your pledge of commitment to overcoming speech anxiety in Exercise 1.3. Reread the goals you recorded in Exercise 2.4. Remind yourself of the commitment you made to those academic, professional, and social goals that overcoming speech anxiety will help you attain.

As with any other meaningful goal in your life, you have to make a commitment to focus your time and energy toward reaching your goal. Decide how much time per week you will devote to overcoming your speech anxiety and stick to it. Be sure to set aside time every day or at least every other day, for learning and practicing the techniques that you scheduled in Exercise 5.5. Most students find that if they are faithful at practicing the techniques and at setting small goals for speaking in public, they will start to notice at least some change in their anxiety level within a few weeks and a major change within a few months.

Conquering speech anxiety is an achievement that comes in increments. The old adage "inch by inch everything's a cinch; yard by yard it's rather hard" certainly applies to this goal. Start with a small, faithful, and consistent commitment of time and energy and you will find yourself feeling a little less anxiety with each practice session. With an internal commitment to overcoming speech anxiety and an external commitment of time and energy, you will make progress.

Kyleen (nurse), age 22, said: "I felt a change in my anxiety level after the first week of practicing my coping statements and deep breathing exercises. I really noticed a big change in how I felt after I practiced SD and gave a three-minute speech of introduction. I would tell everyone to be committed to practicing the techniques regularly. It took a few months, but it changed my life. I no longer feel nervous about giving a speech. I never thought I could ever say this, but I even enjoy giving a speech."

12.2 Check Active Learning

By now, you have at least read through the techniques, but have you taken the time to learn the techniques, really learn them? Active learning means more than passively reading about something. Active learning means that you read and write down responses to the exercises. It means that you record your thoughts about the progress you are making. It means that you work with the techniques until you can apply them at a moment's notice.

Working with the techniques involves following the directions and suggestions in order to get the most benefit out of what the techniques were designed to do for you. Consider the following questions:

- Have you worked with the diaphragmatic breathing exercise so you can use it anytime you feel stressful, even before an exam or job interview, but especially before a speech?

- Have you posted your coping statements list in a conspicuous place where you can read your list often and work at repeating it and memorizing it?

- Are you practicing SD? Did you learn to completely relax using deep muscle relaxation, before you added the visualizations to SD?

- Did you acquire an audio format of the SD and mental rehearsal techniques so that you are faithfully practicing these important techniques by following a professional script?

If you have answered these questions with "yes," and followed the suggestions explained in each chapter, then you are actively learning the techniques. You are and will be experiencing more change in your anxiety level soon.

12.3 Check Your Personal Plan and Practice Schedule

The techniques and exercises presented in this book will work! They have helped thousands of students reduce excessive nervousness and anxiety about public speaking. They will help you too, but **only if you follow your personal plan and practice the techniques.** In Chapter Five, you assessed your BASICS personality dimensions, tracked your firing order, and developed a personal plan for applying speech anxiety techniques that fit your firing order. Your firing order of dimensions is unique to you so you must have a personal plan. When you have applied techniques at every personality dimension involved in your speech anxiety, beginning with the technique that fits the top of your firing order, you will experience a substantial reduction in your fear, nervousness and anxiety about public speaking.

The techniques are a vehicle, like a car that gets you where you want to go but is of little use to you if you leave it parked in the garage. Regularly practicing the techniques will help change your old negative thought patterns, anxious responses, and excessive physical activation into new calm feelings and confident attitudes toward public speaking.

You have lived a long time with your old anxious thought patterns and responses, so they will not disappear overnight or because you practiced a technique once or twice. As mentioned in Part 2 of this book, you will need to practice the techniques until they become more automatic than your old response patterns. "How long will this take for me?" you ask. For each person, the time will vary. Many people start to notice a slight change the first week and experience a little more change with each week of practice until, over a period of a few months, the new calm response patterns are formed. As always, those who experience the most change are those who follow a regular practice schedule and are involved in a public speaking class or workshop where they can practice the techniques along with learning public speaking skills and delivering short speeches.

The best way to stay on track with practicing the techniques is to follow the practice schedule you created in Exercise 5.5. This is part of your commitment to overcoming speech anxiety. If you find yourself not keeping your practice schedule, ask yourself these questions:

1. What is more important than conquering my anxiety or fear about public speaking?

2. Is this alternate activity actually more important than overcoming my communication anxiety?

3. Can I schedule my life so I can practice the techniques and still fulfill all my commitments to other people and activities?

4. What can I cut from my schedule so I can fit the practice sessions into it?

Remember, the person who is going to help you overcome speech anxiety the most is YOU!

The best time to take responsibility to achieve your goals is now. If you take the time to practice these techniques and conquer your speech anxiety, it will be one of the best things you have ever done. Commit yourself to practicing. You can do it!

12.4 Participate in Public Communication

Participating in public communication so you can put your new knowledge, techniques, and skills to use is the final step. If you are not enrolled in a public speaking course or business communication class or workshop, you need to enroll in one soon. As covered in Chapter Eleven, *skills training* is one of the important techniques to learn in conquering speech anxiety. In a public speaking class you will be given many opportunities to learn, practice, and improve your speaking skills.

Many universities offer classes or workshops for individuals who experience public speaking anxiety. These classes often include learning the anxiety-reduction techniques and public speaking skills training, along with numerous opportunities to practice communicating in a supportive environment.

If your local university or community college does not offer a special communication class for those who experience excessive anxiety about public communication, sign up for a public speaking fundamentals class anyway. As soon as you enroll, tell your instructor that you are working on a goal to overcome speech anxiety. Ask for any suggestions the instructor can give you. Show your instructor this book. Continue to work with the techniques presented here. Take advantage of every opportunity to speak. Beginning public speaking classes are truly workshops where many students come with little or no experience and are able to practice in a supportive atmosphere. Also, most beginning public speaking classes will include several students who are apprehensive about public speaking, so you won't be alone. Remember, up to 75 percent of people report fear or anxiety about public speaking. You might even find that you are able to help and support others.

Once you have learned public speaking skills and the techniques to reduce anxiety, use them. The old adage is true, "What you don't use, you lose." The best way to stay confident and to develop more skills is to use what you have. Take advantage of opportunities to speak on the job, in a classroom or as part of a community organization (e.g., Toastmasters International, Rotary, Kiwanis, etc.). This will help you use and develop effective speaking skills.

You now have the tools at hand to conquer your fear and anxiety about public speaking. If you develop a personal plan following the suggestions in this book, you will become a confident speaker. It will be one of the best things you have ever done. Speech anxiety will become a thing of your past, and many wonderful opportunities will be on your horizon.

12.5 A Final Note

This book was written in an effort to help you learn techniques that have been proven to help people who experience public speaking anxiety reduce their anxiety. This book is not meant as a counseling or medical treatment program for those who continue to experience severe anxiety or depression. If you find that you do not get the help you need from practicing the techniques presented in this book, please seek out a counselor or medical professional who is qualified to offer you in-depth anxiety reduction counseling. It is not unusual for individuals who have experienced deep wounds or fears to need counseling in areas beyond speech-anxiety reduction. You have started your journey to conquer speech anxiety by reading this book, so don't be afraid to pursue further goals. Feel empowered to continue to seek any help you need along the path to becoming all you can be!

Journaling #12 Activity: How I See Myself Today

Name   **Date**

Today, you will reflect on your progress toward conquering your speech anxiety. You will assess the changes you have made since you first began your journey. Use the following points to guide your journaling.

1. Describe how you see yourself as a "communicator" now in the following situations:

    a. In everyday conversations

    b. In group discussions

    c. In meetings

    d. In public speaking opportunities

    e. Overall

2. Review how you described yourself as a communicator in Journaling Activity #1 and compare it to how your described yourself today. Recount the changes or improvements you made.

(TEAR-OUT PAGE FOR PRACTICE AND STUDY)

3. Summarize how your body responds to public speaking now (stomach butterflies, racing heart, sweating, blushing, shaking limbs, shivering, feelings of panic or doom, forgetting important points, thinking worrisome or negative thoughts, etc.) then compare it to what you wrote in Journaling Activity #1.

4. Describe the firing order of dimensions involved in your speech anxiety and how you selected treatment techniques based on your firing order.

5. Describe the anxiety reduction techniques that you found most helpful.

6. Describe your anxiety level about giving a speech at this time.

7. Retake the PRCA in Exercise 12.5 and Score it. Then compare your scores to the scores you recorded in Exercise 2.3. Describe the changes in your anxiety level for each context.

(TEAR-OUT PAGE FOR PRACTICE AND STUDY)

Exercise 12.5 Personal Report of Communication Apprehension Survey (PRCA-24)[9]

Name   **Date**

Directions: This instrument is composed of twenty-four statements concerning feelings about communicating with other people. Please indicate in the space provided at the end of each question the degree to which each statement applies to you by marking whether you

(1) Strongly agree, (2) agree, (3) are undecided, (4) disagree, (5) strongly disagree.

1. ___I dislike participating in group discussions.

2. ___Generally, I am comfortable while participating in group discussions.

3. ___I am tense and nervous while participating in group discussions.

4. ___I like to get involved in group discussions.

5. ___Engaging in a group discussion with new people makes me tense and nervous.

6. ___I am calm and relaxed while participating in group discussions.

7. ___Generally, I am nervous when I have to participate in a meeting.

8. ___Usually I am calm and relaxed while participating in a meeting.

9. ___I am very calm and relaxed when I am called upon to express an opinion at a meeting.

10. ___I am afraid to express myself at meetings.

11. ___Communicating at meetings usually makes me uncomfortable.

12. ___I am very relaxed when answering questions at a meeting.

13. ___While participating in a conversation with a new acquaintance, I feel very nervous.

14. ___I have no fear of speaking up in conversations.

15. ___Ordinarily I am very tense and nervous in conversations.

16. ___Ordinarily I am very calm and relaxed in conversations.

17. ___While conversing with a new acquaintance, I feel very relaxed.

18. ___I'm afraid to speak up in conversations.

19. ___I have no fear of giving a speech.

20. ___Certain parts of my body feel very tense and rigid while I am giving a speech.

21. ___I feel relaxed while giving a speech.

22. ___My thoughts become confused and jumbled when I am giving a speech.

23. ___I face the prospect of giving a speech with confidence.

24. ___While giving a speech, I get so nervous I forget facts I really know.

(TEAR-OUT PAGE FOR PRACTICE AND STUDY)

Transfer Your PRCA-24 Survey Scores

To tabulate your scores, you will need to first transfer your survey scores from the previous page to the chart on the next page. So please tear out the previous page and place it next to the chart on the following page to make the transfer and tabulation process easy.

You will use the Norms Chart below after you have transferred and tabulated your scores. Please refer to this page after you have tabulated your scores.

Norms Chart

To interpret your scores, you can compare your scores with the thousands of people who have also completed the PRCA-24. See the following "Norms Chart for the PRCA-24."

Norms Chart for the Prca-24[16]

Context	Average Score	Average Range	High CA Scores
Group	15.4	11 to 20	21 & Above
Meeting	16.4	12 to 21	22 & Above
Conversation	14.5	10 to 18	19 & Above
Pub Speak	19.3	14 to 24	25 & Above
Overall	65.6	50 to 80	81 & Above

Interpret and Compare: Final Assessment

When you have finished tabulating your scores, please describe your progress in conquering anxiety by comparing these scores with your first PRCA-24 scores and anxiety levels in Exercise 2.3

TABULATING YOUR SCORES

Name   **Date**

SCORING: To tabulate your scores, please write your scores from the PRCA-24 survey in the corresponding cells below (next to the appropriate item number in parenthesis). Next add or subtract for each item across each row as indicated. Please note that "18" is a constant so all your sub-scores will be computed by starting with a number of "18 and adding and subtracting as indicated."

Context	ADD scores to 18 for item numbers				MINUS scores for item numbers				Context Scores
Group	18	+(2)___	+(4)___	+(6)___	=___	-(1)___	-(3)___	-(5)___	=_____
Meetings	18	+(2)___	+(4)___	+(6)___	=___	-(1)___	-(3)___	-(5)___	=_____
Conver-sations	18	+(2)___	+(4)___	+(6)___	=___	-(1)___	-(3)___	-(5)___	=_____
Public Speaking	18	+(2)___	+(4)___	+(6)___	=___	-(1)___	-(3)___	-(5)___	=_____
Overall	**Add all Four Context Subscores for an overall score=>**								

Your Scores Chart (Write your scores in the chart below . Compare them to the Norms Chart on the previous page. Next check (√) your anxiety level based on the Norms Chart.)

CONTEXT & OVERALL	**YOUR SCORES**	**CHECK (√) YOUR LEVEL**		
		Low	Average	High
Group				
Meetings				
Conversations				
Public Speaking				
Overall				

Chapter Summary

You can conquer your speech anxiety by putting together all that you have learned into a personal plan. You will need to commit yourself to the goal of overcoming speech anxiety; check your progress at actively learning the techniques targeted to your firing order; check your practice schedule to ensure you are practicing the techniques regularly; and participate in public communication so you can put your new knowledge, techniques, and skills to use. The person who is going to help you the most in conquering speech anxiety is you. The best time to take responsibility to achieve your goals is now. If you take the time to follow an action plan to conquer your speech anxiety, it will be one of the best things you have ever done. Keep pursuing your goals and getting the help you need.

Review Questions

After reading this chapter, you should be able to answer the following:

1. Explain the four measures for developing an action plan to overcome speech anxiety.
2. What does active learning mean in reference to overcoming speech anxiety?
3. Is there a miracle cure for speech anxiety? How long will it take to see results?
4. What is the best way to begin participating in public communication?

Notes

[1]Reprinted by permission of the author, Dr. James C. McCroskey. McCroskey, 1998.

Congratulations!

YOU ARE ON THE PATH TO BECOMING A CONFIDENT SPEAKER!

Personal Notes

Appendix 1

Script for Learning Progressive Muscle Relaxation

You can use the iConquer Speech Anxiety MP3 (see www.iconquerspeechanxiety.com)to practice Systematic Desensitization and Progressive Muscle Relation or you can create your own recording. It is imperative that you have a recording to lead you through this technique. To create your own, use a recorder and try to speak in a calm and relaxed voice. Follow this script. (The time in parentheses is meant as a guide to tell you how long to pause before continuing. Do not speak the time aloud.)

- With your eyes closed, take three deep abdominal diaphragmatic breaths. Inhale deeply (pause five seconds). Exhale slowly through the mouth. Take another deep breath; hold it (pause five seconds). Now exhale slowly. Again, inhale deeply and hold it (pause five seconds). Exhale slowly and completely. Begin to concentrate on letting go of all tension.

- Now, try to concentrate on each part of your body. Beginning with your left hand, tightly clench your left fist. Hold your muscles very tightly, but not so tightly that it is uncomfortable. Study the tension in your left hand and forearm. Note how strained these muscles feel (pause five seconds).

- Now relax your left hand. Let it relax very comfortably on your lap or on the arm of your chair. Note how pleasant relaxation feels and how it contrasts with the tension (pause ten seconds).

- Again tightly clench your left fist. Hold your muscles very tightly. Study the tension and hold it (pause five seconds).

- Relax your hand. Let your left hand open and get very relaxed. Notice the pleasant feeling of relaxation in your left hand and how it contrasts with the tension (pause ten seconds).

- Now with your right hand, tightly clench your fist. Study the tension in your right hand and in your fore-arm. Note how strained the muscles feel (pause five seconds).

- Now relax. Let your right hand open up so that even your fingers feel relaxed (pause ten seconds).

- Again, clench your right fist. Your muscles feel tense, but not painful. Study the tension in your hand (pause five seconds). Now relax your right hand. Open up the fingers on your right hand. Note how relaxation feels (pause ten seconds).

- Now with your left hand resting on your lap or arm of a chair, bend your hand backward at the wrist, toward your shoulders so that your fingers are pointing to your face. Study the tension in your hand and forearm (pause five seconds).

- Relax those muscles. Notice how pleasant relaxation feels in contrast to tenseness (pause ten seconds).

- Again with your left hand, point your fingers backward and toward your shoulders.

- You should feel the tension in the back of your hand. Study the tension (pause five seconds).

- Relax your hand once again on your lap or chair. Notice how pleasant relaxation feels (pause ten seconds).

- Now with your right hand resting on your lap or arm of a chair, bend it at the wrist, pointing it backward toward your shoulders. Study the tension in the back of your hand and forearm (pause five seconds). Let your hand fully relax on your lap or chair. Notice the difference between tension and relaxation (pause ten seconds).

- Again, bend your right hand at the wrist and point it backward toward your shoulders. Study the tension and hold it (pause five seconds). Relax the right hand. Let it go loose and limp. Note the feelings of relaxation (pause ten seconds).

- Now with both arms, tense your biceps by bringing your forearms toward your shoulders and making a muscle with both arms. Study the tension in your forearms (pause five seconds).

- Relax. Drop your arms to your chair or your thighs and note how pleasant it feels to release the tension (pause ten seconds).

- Again tense your biceps by bringing your forearms up toward your shoulders and making a muscle with both arms. Feel the tension (pause five seconds).

- Relax. Drop your arms back to your lap or chair. Note how very pleasant it feels to release the tension (pause ten seconds).

- Next, shrug both shoulders. Tighten your shoulders by raising them up as if you are going to touch your ears. Note the tension in your shoulders, in your neck, and in your back. Study the tension (pause five seconds).

- Relax your shoulder muscles. Note how relaxed you feel (pause ten seconds).

- Shrug your shoulders again. Raise them way up and feel the tension in your shoulders and neck and back (pause five seconds).

- Relax them again and notice how very pleasant it feels to release the tension (pause ten seconds).

- Tense your muscles in your forehead by raising your eyebrows as much as you can. Study the tension around your eyes and above your eyes and forehead (pause five seconds).

- Smooth out your forehead muscles. They are feeling relaxed (pause ten seconds).

- Now again, tense the muscles in your forehead by raising your eyebrows as much as you can. Study those tensions (pause five seconds).

- Relax the forehead muscles. Smooth them out. Notice how very pleasant it feels to release the tension and enjoy the relaxation (pause ten seconds).

- Next, tense the muscles around your eyes by closing your eyes very tightly. Study the tension (pause five seconds).

- Relax. Your eyes remain lightly closed and relaxed (pause ten seconds).

- Again, clench your eyelids very tightly. Hold it (pause five seconds).

- Relax those muscles around your eyes. Notice how pleasant it feels to release the tension around your eyes (pause ten seconds).

- Now press your tongue firmly into the roof of your mouth. Tighten all those muscles in your mouth and hold it (pause five seconds).

- Let your tongue drop in your mouth to a very relaxed position. Notice how relaxed your mouth and tongue feel (pause ten seconds).

- Again, press your tongue firmly into the roof of your mouth. Study the tension (pause five seconds).

- Relax those muscles that control your tongue (pause ten seconds).

- Next press your lips together. Study the tension around your mouth (pause five seconds).

- Relax the muscles around your mouth. Note how pleasant it feels to relax the mouth (pause ten seconds).

- Again press your lips together. Study the tension (pause five seconds).

- Relax those muscles. Your lips will come apart slightly (pause ten seconds).

- Next, tighten the muscles in the back of your neck, pushing your head back as far as you can against the chair or until you can feel tension on your neck. Study the tension in your neck (pause five seconds).

- Relax and let your head come forward to a resting position. Feel that relaxation flowing into your entire neck area and throat (pause ten seconds).

- Again, push your head back against the chair. Study the tension in the back of your neck (pause five seconds).

- Relax those neck muscles. Feel the relaxation flowing into your neck as your head comes forward to the resting position (pause ten seconds).

- Now bring your chin forward as if to bury it in your chest. Study the tension in the front of the neck (pause five seconds).

- Relax by returning your head to its resting position. Notice how pleasant relaxation feels as tension is released (pause ten seconds).

- Again, bring your chin forward until it is almost buried in your chest. Study the tension in the front of your neck (pause five seconds).

- Relax. Notice how pleasant it feels to relax (pause ten seconds).

- Next, arch your back. Stick out your chest and lift your back off of your chair. Study the tension in your back (pause five seconds).

- Relax. Notice the contrast between the tension and the comfortable feeling of relaxation (pause ten seconds).

- Again, arch your back, way back, lifting your back off the chair. Study the tension (pause five seconds).

- Relax. You feel all tension leaving your body and relaxation spreading to every muscle (pause ten seconds).

- Tighten the muscles in your chest by taking a very deep breath. Hold it and study the tension in your chest (pause five seconds).

- Exhale and relax (pause ten seconds).

- Again, take a deep breath so that your abdomen rises instead of your chest. Hold it and study the tension (pause five seconds).

- Exhale and relax (pause ten seconds).

- Now, take a deep breath in through your nose and tighten your stomach as tight as you can and hold it (pause five seconds).

- Relax your stomach. Note the difference between tension and the feelings of relaxation (pause ten seconds).

- Tense your stomach muscles one more time. Breathe in through your nose and tighten your stomach as much as you can. Hold it as tight as you can and study the tension (pause five seconds).

- Relax your stomach muscles. Feel the relaxation spreading into your stomach area. Your breathing has returned to normal (pause ten seconds).

- Now tense your buttocks by pushing them into the seat of your chair. Feel the tension. Hold that position (pause five seconds).

- Relax those muscles. Notice the contrast between tension and relaxation (pause ten seconds).

- Again, push your seat into your chair. Study the tension and hold it (pause five seconds).

- Relax those muscles (pause ten seconds).

- Now squeeze the thigh muscles in both of your legs by straightening both legs and lifting your feet off the floor. Study the tension in your thigh muscles and hold it (pause five seconds).

- Relax and let your feet drop (pause ten seconds).

- Again, squeeze your thigh muscles. Straighten both legs and stretch them out as far as you can (pause five seconds).

- Relax your thighs (pause ten seconds).

- Next, bend your feet and toes up toward the ceiling, tensing the muscles in the calves and ankles. Hold it (pause five seconds).

- Relax. Let the muscles in your calves get very loose and relaxed (pause ten seconds).

- Again, tense your calf muscles by bending your feet upward toward the ceiling. Notice how strained the muscles feel (pause five seconds).

- Let go and relax. Feel the relaxation coming into your calf muscles (pause ten seconds).

- Curl the toes of both feet under and tense your arch area so you can feel the tension in the arch of your foot. Study that tension (pause five seconds).

- Relax. Notice how pleasant relaxation feels in contrast to the tension (pause ten seconds).

- Again, curl the toes of both feet under. Study the tension in your feet and in your arches (pause five seconds).

- Relax and enjoy the calmness (pause ten seconds).

- Now go back through several muscle groups that you have been relaxing. When each muscle group is mentioned, make sure it is relaxed.

- Relax both hands (pause ten seconds).

- Relax your forearms and upper arms (pause ten seconds).

- Relax your shoulders and neck (pause ten seconds).

- Relax your forehead and facial muscles (pause ten seconds).

- Relax your mouth (pause ten seconds).

- Feel the relaxation spreading from your head and neck to your chest and stomach (pause ten seconds).

- Relaxation is spreading to your buttocks (pause ten seconds). Relax your thighs (pause ten seconds).

- Relax your calves and feet (pause ten seconds).

You have just completed the deep muscle relaxation phase in SD. Slowly open your eyes, and then shut the tape off.

You should practice with your recording until your body is very familiar with relaxation. You want your body to be able to relax on demand, so it will take a few days of practice to train your body to quickly bring your muscles to a feeling of deep relaxation.

(Note: You should practice progressive muscle relaxation at least two times or until you can completely relax your body using this method. Then you are ready to add the first four mental pictures from your hierarchy of anxious events. You will say the following visualizations with pauses.)

1. Thinking about the speech you will give while sitting in your room alone (hold 15 seconds)

2. Sitting in the room where you are being asked to give a speech (hold 15 seconds)

3. Reading a book about planning and delivering a speech (hold 15 seconds

4. Receiving a formal speaking request or assignment (hold 15 seconds)

(NOTE: You should try to hold the mental picture of each situation for at least fifteen seconds while maintaining complete relaxation. If any muscle becomes tense, clear your mind of the mental picture and concentrate on relaxing that muscle. When all muscles are relaxed, try again to hold the mental picture and maintain complete relaxation for at least fifteen seconds. Do not move on to visualizing the next situation until you can maintain complete relaxation with the previous situation on your hierarchy. Once you have visualized all of the four lowest anxiety-provoking situations from your hierarchy of events, take a few deep breaths, open your eyes, and become aware of your surroundings again and STOP practice. You should practice with only four new mental pictures at a time in order to give your mind and body a chance to bond relaxation with the mental pictures.)

For the next SD practice session, listen to the relaxation recording. Check to see if you can maintain relaxation with the first four mental pictures. If you can, move on to visualizing each of the next four situations from your hierarchy of anxious events.

For example, you could add the following visualizations.

1. Preparing your speech by writing your speech outline (hold 15 seconds)

2. Rehearsing your speech alone in your room (hold 15 seconds)

3. Rising and getting dressed on the day of the speech (hold 15 seconds)

4. Walking to the room and entering it on the day of your speech (hold 15 seconds)

(Again, when you can maintain complete relaxation for at least fifteen seconds with each situation, take a few deep breaths, open your eyes, and become aware of your surroundings. At your next session, you will again listen to the relaxation part of the recording. Check to see if you can maintain relaxation with the previous four mental pictures. If you can, move on to visualizing each of the final four situations from your hierarchy of anxious events. For example, you could add the final visualizations.)

1. Waiting to give your speech while another person introduces you or speaks (hold 15 seconds)

2. Walking up before your audience (hold 15 seconds)

3. Presenting your speech before the audience and seeing the faces looking at you (hold 15 seconds)

4. Fielding questions after your speech and then walking back to your seat filled with energy and confidence (hold 15 seconds)

    (Again, when you can maintain complete relaxation for at least fifteen seconds with each situation, take a few deep breaths, open your eyes, and become aware of your surroundings.)

Personal Notes

Appendix 2

Script for the Mental Rehearsal Technique

You can use the iConquer Speech Anxiety MP3 (see www.iconquerspeechanxiety.com) to practice **Mental Rehearsal** or you can create your own recording. Use a recorder and try to speak in a calm and relaxed voice in order to make your own recording. Follow this script, which is based on a visualization script for public speaking suggested by Ayres and Hopf1. (The time in parentheses is meant as a guide to tell you how long to pause before continuing. Do not speak the time aloud.)

- Try to become as comfortable as possible in your chair. Position your hands on your lap or on the arms of the chair so they feel relaxed. Remove your glasses, if you like, in order to get more comfortable. Close your eyes. Move around until you feel comfortable.

- Take a deep abdominal diaphragmatic breath so that your abdomen rises, not your chest. Hold it. (Pause five seconds.) Slowly release it.

- Take another deep abdominal breath. Hold it. (Pause five seconds.) Slowly release it. Note how good you feel while you are breathing deeply. Feel the relaxation starting to flow through the limbs of your body to your fingers and toes.

- Take another deep, comfortable breath. Hold it for a few seconds. (Pause five seconds.) Slowly release it.

- Now return to your normal breathing pattern. Again, try to get as comfortable as you can in your chair.

- Begin to mentally picture the dawn of the day on which you are going to give your speech. Try to picture the day just as it will be when you arise. You have had a very restful night. See yourself getting out of bed in the morning. You feel energized and confident. You say to yourself, "I am prepared to meet the challenges of this day; I am looking forward to sharing my ideas with my friends or colleagues." (Pause five seconds.)

- See yourself taking the clothes out of your closet that you think are right for your plans for the day and will help you feel good about yourself. As you are dressing, you notice that you have a very positive attitude. You say, "I believe in myself and my goals to help others." (Pause five seconds.) Try to picture any activities you usually do before you leave in the morning. (Pause five seconds.)

- Next, see yourself driving or riding or biking or walking to the place where you will be giving your presentation. See yourself smiling as you practice the diaphragmatic breathing exercises on the way. Note how self- assured you feel. You have worked hard to prepare and rehearse your speech. You have practiced your positive coping statements and you feel very positive about this task. (Pause five seconds.)

- See yourself walking into the building and then into the room where you will speak. Those in the room appear warm and friendly. They greet you with very positive remarks.

- One person says she's been looking forward to hearing your speech. Another tells you they are eager to listen to your message. (Pause five seconds.)

- You feel thoroughly prepared to speak as you walk over to your seat. You are mentally and physically ready for the occasion. You have thoroughly researched your topic and all your materials. Your outline is complete. Because of your rehearsing, you are confident about the timing and flow of words. You are prepared in every way for what you are presenting today. You are calm, yet ready. You say to yourself: "I appreciate my efforts; I know I can provide ideas that will be helpful to some." (Pause five seconds.)

- See yourself sitting at your seat in the classroom. You are conversing very comfortably and confidently with those around you. You assure others that you are looking forward to hearing from them or meeting with them. You feel absolutely confident about your presentation and your ability to deliver your speech in a lively and confident manner. You know your message will be beneficial to many in your listeners. (Pause five seconds.)

- It is now approaching your time to speak. As you wait, see yourself taking a relaxed deep abdominal breath and saying: "My audience wants me to succeed. I will do the best I can to offer the ideas I have prepared." (Pause five seconds.)

- Next, see yourself moving to the front of the room. You are feeling very positive about your presentation. You are well organized and well planned and ready to go. (Pause five seconds.)

- Visualize yourself delivering your presentation. You're really quite good. You notice that your audience is giving you positive feedback with head nods, eye contact, and smiles. They are conveying the message: They are with you, and they are interested in what you are saying. You are helping them. (Pause five seconds.)

- Your attention-getter and opening remarks go the way you have planned. You establish your credibility and preview your points. You move smoothly into the body of your speech. Your first main point comes forth just as you had planned. The evidence that you use— stories, examples, quotations and statistics help make your points. You can see that you have your audience's attention and interest. (Pause five seconds.)

- See yourself unfolding each of your main points smoothly. Your words come easily as in everyday conversation. You are passionate and use natural gestures and vocal inflections to emphasize your points. Now, see yourself finishing the points in the body of your speech and moving to the ending. You summarize the main points, and end in a memorable way so that the conclusion is a fitting finale to your speech.

- When you have finished your last few words, you say to yourself: "This presentation went very well. I am pleased with myself and my speech. The introduction invited my audience into the topic. My main points were clear and easy to follow. My evidence and stories was convincing. My conclusion was an appealing and fitting end to my entire speech. I used inflections to convey my enthusiasm and commitment. I paused to emphasize important ideas. I used gestures and body movements in a natural way. See yourself receiving applause. People express their appreciation. A few raise their hands to ask questions, which you confidently answer--or you make suggestions about where they could go for additional information. (Pause five seconds.)

- You are relaxed and gratified. You accomplished your goal of sharing your ideas with others. You have done a good job and you feel it. You are energized and ready for the rest of your day. Giving a presentation has been a truly fulfilling and confidence-building experience for you. You can look forward to another presentation or other new challenges.

- Begin to return your thoughts to this time and this place. Take a deep abdominal diaphragmatic breath. Hold it. (Pause five seconds.)

- Let it go. Again, take a really deep abdominal breath. Hold it. (Pause five seconds.) Exhale. Do this a few more times. (Pause five seconds.)

- Get ready to open your eyes. Take as much time as you need to transition back to this time and place. Now open your eyes. You are ready to go!

Notes

[1] Ayers & Hopf, 1989

Reference List

Addison, P., Ayala, J., Hunter, M., Behnke, R. R., & Sawyer, C. R. (2004). Body sensations of higher and lower anxiety sensitive speakers anticipating a public presentation. *Communication Research Reports, 21*, 284_290.

Addison, P., Clay, E., Xie, S., Sawyer, C. R., & Behnke, R. R. (2003). Worry as a function of public speaking anxiety type. *Communication Reports, 16*, 125_131.

Allen, M. T. (1989). A comparison of self-report, observer, and physiological assessments of public speaking anxiety reduction techniques using meta-analysis. *Communication Studies, 40*, 127-139.

Allen, M., Hunter, J., & Donohue, W. (1989). Meta-analysis of self-report data on the effectiveness of public speaking anxiety treatment techniques. *Communication Education, 38*, 54–76.

Anthony, W. P., Maddox, E. N., & Wheatley, W. (1988). *Envisionary management*. New York: Quorum Books.

Assagioli, R. (1973). *The act of will*. New York: Viking Press.

Assagioli, R. (1976). *Psychosynthesis: A manual of principles and techniques*. New York: Penguin Books.

Ayres, J. (1986). Perceptions of speaking ability: An explanation of stage fright. *Communication Education, 35*, 275–287.

Ayres, J. (1988). Antecedents of communication apprehension: A reaffirmation. *Communication Research Reports, 5*, 58–63.

Ayres, J. (1991). Using visual aids to reduce speech anxiety. *Communication Research Reports*, 8, 73–79. Ayres, J. (1994). Effective public speaking. Madison, WI: WCB Brown & Benchmark.

Ayres, J., & Hopf, T. S. (1985). Visualization: A means of reducing speech anxiety. *Communication Education, 35*, 318–323.

Ayres, J., & Hopf, T. S. (1989). Is it more than extra-attention? *Communication Education, 38*, 1–5.

Ayres, J., & Hopf, T. S. (1991). Coping with writing apprehension. *Journal of Applied Communication Research, 19*, 318–323.

Ayres, J., & Hopf, T. S. (1993). *Coping with speech anxiety.* Norwood, NJ: Ablex.

Ayres, J., Hopf, T., & Ayres, D. M. (1994). An examination of whether imaging ability enhances the effectiveness of an intervention designed to reduce speech anxiety. *Communication Education, 73*, 252-258.

Ayres, J., Hopf, T., Hazel, M. T., Sonandre, D. M., & Wongprasert, T. K. (2009). Visualization and performance visualization: Applications, evidence, and speculation. In J.A. Daly, J.C. McCroskey, J. Ayres, T. Hopf, D. Sonandre, & T. A. Wongprasert (Eds.), *Avoiding Communication: Shyness, Reticence, and Communication Apprehension* (pp. 375-394). Cresskill, NJ: Hampton Press.

Ayres, J., Hopf, T., & Edwards, P. A. (1999). Vividness and control: Factors in the effectiveness of performance visualization. *Communication Education, 48*, 287-293.

Ayres, J., Hopf, T., & Nagami, K. (1999). A test of COM therapy in Japan. *Communication Research Reports, 16*, 317-324.

Ayres, J., Hopf, T., & Peterson, E. (2000). A test of Communication-Orientation Motivation (COM) therapy. *Communication Reports, 13*, 35-44.

Bandura, A. (1973). *Social learning theory.* Englewood Cliffs, NJ: Prentice Hall.

Beck, J. S. & Beck, A. T. (2011). *Cognitive behavior therapy; Basics & beyond.* New York: Guilford.

Beck, A. T., Rush, A. J., Shaw, B. F., & Emery, G. (1979). *Cognitive therapy of depression.* New York: Guilford.

Behnke, R. R., & Beatty, L. W. (1981). A cognitive-physiological model of speech anxiety. *Communication Monographs, 48*, 158–163.

Behnke, R. R., & Sawyer, C. R. (1999). Milestones of anticipatory public speaking anxiety. *Communication Education, 48*, 165_172.

Behnke, R. R., & Sawyer, C. R. (2000). Anticipatory anxiety patterns for male and female public speakers. *Communication Education, 49*, 187-195.

Behnke, R. R., & Sawyer, C. R. (2001a). Patterns of psychological state anxiety in public speaking as a function of anxiety sensitivity. *Communication Quarterly, 49*, 84-94.

Behnke, R. R., & Sawyer, C. R. (2001b). Public speaking arousal as a function of anticipatory activation and autonomic reactivity. *Communication Reports, 14*, 73_85.

Behnke, R. R., & Sawyer, C. R. (2004). Public speaking anxiety as a function of sensitization and habituation processes. *Communication Education, 53*, 164-173.

Benson, H. (1975). *The relaxation response.* New York: William Morrow and Company.

Benson, H., & Klipper, M. Z. (2000). *The relaxation response.* New York: William Morrow and Company.

Booth-Butterfield, M., & Booth-Butterfield, S. (1993). The role of cognitive performance orientation in communication anxiety. *Communication Quarterly, 41*, 198-209.

Booth-Butterfield, M., & Booth-Butterfield, S. (2001). *Communication apprehension and avoidance in the classroom.* Edina, MN: Burgess Publishing.

Bourne E. (2005, 2001). *The Anxiety and Phobia Workbook.* Oakland, CA: New Harbinger Publications.

Bruskin Report (1973, July). *What are Americans afraid of?* (Research Rep. No. 53).

Burns, D. (1999). *Feeling good: The new mood therapy.* New York: William Morrow and Company.

Burns, D. (2007). *When panic attacks: The new, drug-free anxiety therapy that can change your life.* New York: Three Rivers Press

Cannon, W. B. (1914). The emergency function of the adrenal medulla in pain and the major emotions. *American Journal of Physiology, 33*, 356–372.

Clark, L. V. (1960). Effect of mental practice on the development of a certain motor skill. *Research Quarterly of the American Association for Health, Physical Education, & Recreation, 31*, 1960, 560-569.

Clevenger, T., & King, T. R. (1961). A factor analysis of the visible symptoms of stage fright. *Speech Monographs, 25*, 296–298.

Daly, J. A., & Buss A. H. (1984). *The transitory causes of audience anxiety.* In J. A. Daly and J. C. McCroskey (Eds.), Avoiding communication. Beverly Hills, CA: Sage.

Daly, J. G., Caughlin, J. P. & Stafford, L. (2009). Correlates and consequences of social-communicative anxiety. In J.A. Daly, J.C. McCroskey, J. Ayres, T. Hopf, D. Sonandre, & T. A. Wongprasert (Eds.), *Avoiding Communication: Shyness, Reticence, and Communication Apprehension* (pp. 23-52). Cresskill, NJ: Hampton Press.

Daniels, K., & Guppy, A. (1994). Occupational stress, social support, job control, and psychological wellbeing. *Human Relations, 47*, 1523–1544.

Davis, M., Eshelman, E. & McKay, M. (2000). *The relaxation and stress workbook.* Oakland, CA: New Harbinger Publications.

Desberg, P. & Marsh, G. (1988). *Controlling stagefright: Presenting yourself to audiences from one to one thousand.* Oakland, CA: New Harbinger Publications.

Driskell, J., Copper, C., & Moran, A. (1994). Does mental practice enhance performance? *Journal of Applied Psychology, 79*(4), 481-492. doi:10.1037/0021-9010.79.4.481

Dryden & Ellis, A. (2010). *The Practice of Rational Emotive Therapy.* New York; Springer Publishing Company.

Dryden, W., DiGiuseppe, R., & Neenan, M. (2002). *A primer on rational-emotive therapy.* Champaign, IL: Research Press.

Duff, D. C., Levine, T. R., Beatty, M. J., Woolbright, J., & Park, H. S. (2007). Testing public speaking anxiety treatments against a credible placebo control. Communication Education, 56, 72-88.

Dwyer, K. (1995). Creating and teaching special sections of a public speaking course for apprehensive students: A multi-case study. Basic *Communication Course Annual, 7,* 100–124.

Dwyer, K. (1998). Communication apprehension and learning style preference: Correlations and implications for teaching. *Communication Education, 47* (2), 101–114.

Dwyer, K. (1998). *Conquer your speechfright.* Fort Worth: Harcourt Brace.

Dwyer, K. (1998). *Instructor's manual and test bank for conquer your speechfright.* Fort Worth: Harcourt Brace.

Dwyer, K. (2000). The multidimensional model: Teaching students to self-manage high communication apprehension by self-selecting treatments. *Communication Education, 49,* 72–81.

Dwyer, K. (2005). *Conquer your speech anxiety.* New York: Wadsworth.

Dwyer, K. (2005). Instructor's manual and test bank for conquer your speech anxiety. New York: Wadsworth.

Dwyer, K. (2009). The Multidimensional Model for Selecting Interventions. In J.A. Daly, J.C. McCroskey, J. Ayres, T. Hopf, D. Sonandre, & T. A. Wongprasert (Eds.), *Avoiding Communication: Shyness, Reticence, and Communication Apprehension* (pp. 359-374). Cresskill, NJ: Hampton Press.

Dwyer, K. (2012). i*Conquer your speech anxiety.* Kindle Edition: Amazon.com.

Dwyer, K. (2012). iConquer Speech Anxiety. http://www.iconquerspeechanxiety.com.

Dwyer, K. & Davidson, M. (2012). Is public speaking really more feared than death? *Communication Research Reports, 29*: 2, 99-107.

Dwyer, K. (2012). *Public Speaking Student Workbook.* (240 pg.). Boston: Pearson

Dwyer, K. & Fus, D. (2002). Perceptions of communication competence, self-efficacy, and trait communication apprehension: Is there an impact on basic course success? *Communication Research Reports, 19* (1), 29–37.

Dwyer, K. & Fus, D. (1999). Communication apprehension, self-efficacy, and grades in the basic course: Correlations and implications. *Basic Communication Course Annual* 11, 108–132.

Dwyer, K. & Cruz, A. (1998). Communication apprehension, personality, and grades in the basic course: Are there correlations. *Communication Research Reports, 15* (4), 436–444.

Dwyer, K., & Baartmans, T. (2003). *Vanzelfsprekend. (Speak for yourself).* Lisse, The Netherlands: Swets & Zeitlinger Publishers (Taylor & Francis Group, 2012)

Dwyer, K., Carlson, R. E., & Dalbey, J. (2003). Impact of high school preparation on college oral communication apprehension. Basic *Communication Course Annual 15*, 17–113.

Dwyer, K., Carlson, R. E., & Kahre, S. (2002). Communication apprehension and basic course success: The lab-supported public speaking course intervention. *Basic Communication Course Annual 14*, 87–112.

Ellis, A. (2001). *Overcoming destructive beliefs, feelings, and behaviors: New directions for Rational Emotive Behavior Therapy.* Amherst, NY, US: Prometheus Books.

Ellis, A., & Dryden, W. (1987). *The practice of rational emotive therapy.* New York: Springer Publishing.

Ellis, A., & Harper, R. E. (1975). *A new guide to rational living.* North Hollywood, CA: Wilshire Book.

Evans, L., Jones, L., Mullen, R. (2004). An imagery intervention during the competitive season with an elite rugby union player. *The Sport Psychologist, 18*, 252-271

Fanning, P. (1988). *Visualization for change.* Oakland, CA: New Harbinger.

Fawcett, S. B., & Miller, L. K. (1975). Training public speaking behavior: An experimental analysis and social validation. *Journal of Applied Behavior Analysis, 8*,125–135.

Finn, A. N., Sawyer, C. R., & Behnke, R. R. (2009). A model of anxious arousal for public speaking. *Communication Education, 58*(3), 417-432.

Finn, A. N., Sawyer, C. R., Schrodt, P. (2009). Examining the effect of exposure therapy on public speaking state. *Communication Education, 58*(1), 417-432.

Fremouw, W. J., & Zitter, R. E. (1978). A comparison of skills training and cognitive restructuring-relaxation for the treatment of speech anxiety. *Behavior Therapy, 9*, 248–259.

Friedrich, G., Goss, B., Cunconan, T. & Lane, D. (1997). Systematic desensitization. In J.A. Daly & J.C. McCroskey (Eds.), *Avoiding communication* (2nd ed.). Beverly Hills, CA: Sage.

Lane, D., B., G., Cunconan, T., Friedrich, G., & Goss, B. (2009). Systematic desensitization. In J.A. Daly, J.C. McCroskey, J. Ayres, T. Hopf, D. Sonandre, & T. A. Wongprasert (Eds.), *Avoiding Communication: Shyness, Reticence, and Communication Apprehension* (pp. 257-274). Cresskill, NJ: Hampton Press.

Garfield, C. (1984). *Peak performance.* Los Angeles: Jeremy P. Tarcher, Inc.

German, L., Dwyer, K., Denker, K., Milleman, K., Allen, E., Anderson, K., Culiver, G. (2003). *Deep abdominal breathing: A new treatment for moderate public speaking anxiety.* Paper presented at the annual meeting of the National Communication Association, Miami.

Gilkerson, H. (1942). Social fears as reported by students in college speech classes. *Speech Monographs, 9*, 141–160.

Glaser, S. R. (1981). Oral communication apprehension and avoidance: The current status of treatment research. *Communication Education, 30*, 321–341.

Greenberg, J. S. (2003). *Comprehensive stress management.* New York: McGraw-Hill.

Hopf, T., & Ayres, J. (1992). Coping with public speaking anxiety: An examination of various combinations of systematic desensitization, skills training, and visualization. *Journal of Applied Communication Research 20*, 183-198.

Horvath, N. R., Moss, M. N., Xie, S., Sawyer, C. R., & Behnke, R. R. (2004). Evaluation sensitivity and physical sensations of stress as components of public speaking state anxiety. *Southern Communication Journal, 69*, 173-181.

Howe, M. & Dwyer, K. (2007). The influence of diaphragmatic breathing to reduce situational anxiety for basic course students. *Basic Communication Course Annual 19*,104-137.

Jacobs, E. E., Harvill, R. L., & Masson, R. L. (1988). *Group counseling strategies and skills.* Pacific Grove, CA: Brooks/Cole Publishing Company.

Jacobs, E.E., Masson, R. L., Harvill, R. L., Schimmel, C. J. (2012). *Group counseling: Strategies and skills.* Belmont, CA: Brooks/Cole.

Jacobson, E. (1938). *Progressive relaxation.* Chicago: Chicago University Press.

Jordet, G. (2005). Perceptual training in soccer: An imagery intervention study with elite players. *Journal of Applied Sport Psychology, 17*, 140-156.

Kagan, J., & Reznick, J. (1986). Shyness and temperament. In W. Jones, J. Cheek, & S. Briggs (Eds.), *Shyness: Perspectives on research and treatment* (pp. 81–90). New York: Plenum Press.

Kagan, J., Reznick, J., & Snidman, N. (1988). Biological bases of childhood shyness. *Science, 240*, 167–171.

Kelly, L. (1989). Implementing a skills training program for reticent communicators. *Communication Education, 38*, 85–101.

Kelly, L, & Keaten, J. (2000). Effectiveness of the Penn State program in changing beliefs associated with reticence. *Communication Education, 49*, 134–146.

Kelly, L. & Keaten, J. A. (2009). Skills training as a treatment for communication problems. In J.A. Daly, J.C. McCroskey, J. Ayres, T. Hopf, D. Sonandre, & T. A. Wongprasert (Eds.), *Avoiding Communication: Shyness, Reticence, and Communication Apprehension* (pp. 293-326). Cresskill, NJ: Hampton Press.

Kelly, L., Duran, R., & Stewart, J. (1990). Rhetoritherapy revisited: A test of its effectiveness as a treatment for communication problems. *Communication Education, 39*, 207–266.

Kelly, L., Phillips, G M., & Keaten, J. A. (1995). *Teaching people to speak well.* Cresskill, NJ:

Hampton Press. Kendall, G., Hrycaiko, D., Martin, G. L., & Kendall, T. (1990). The effects of an imagery rehearsal, relaxation, and self-talk package on basketball game performance. *Journal of Sport and Exercise Psychology, 12*, 157-166.

Lakey, B. (2010). Social support: Basic research and new strategies for intervention. In J. E. Maddux & J.P. Tangney (Eds.) *Social Psychological Foundations of Clinical Psychology* (pp. 177 – 194). NY: Guildford.

Lane, D. R., Cunconan, T. M., Friedrich, G. (2009). Systematic desensitization. In J.A. Daly, J.C. McCroskey, J. Ayres, T. Hopf, D. Sonandre, & T. A. Wongprasert (Eds.*), Avoiding Communication: Shyness, Reticence, and Communication Apprehension* (pp. 275-292). Cresskill, NJ: Hampton Press.

Lazarus, A. (1978). What is multimodal therapy? A brief overview. *Elementary School Guidance and Counseling, 10,* 6–29.

Lazarus, A. (1989). *The practice of multimodal therapy.* Baltimore, MD: John Hopkins University Press.

Lazarus, A. (1997). Brief but comprehensive psychotherapy: The multimodal way. New York: Springer. Levine, T. R., & McCroskey, J. C. (1990). Measuring trait communication apprehension: A test of rival measurement models of the PRCA 24. *Communication Monographs, 57* (1) 62-72.

Levine, P.A. (1997). *Waking the tiger. Berkeley California.* North Atlantic Books.

Lucas, S. E. (2012). *The art of public speaking.* New York: McGraw-Hill.

M. Burgoon (Ed.) (1981), *Communication yearbook, 5.* New Brunswick, NJ: Transaction Books.

Manchester, W. (1967). *The death of a president,* November 20-November 25. New York: Harper & Row.

McCroskey, J. C. (1972). The implementation of a large-scale program of systematic desensitization for communication apprehension. *Speech Teacher, 21,* 255–264.

McCroskey, J. C. (1977). Oral communication apprehension: A review of recent theory and research. *Human Communication Research, 4,* 78–96.

McCroskey, J. C. (1982). Oral communication apprehension: A reconceptualization. In M. Burgoon (Ed.), *Communication yearbook 6.* Beverly Hills, CA: Sage.

McCroskey, J. C., Richmond, R., & McCroskey, L. (2009). Willingness to communicate, communication apprehension, and self-perceived communication competence: Conceptualizations and perspectives. In J.A. Daly, J.C. McCroskey, J. Ayres, T. Hopf, D. Sonandre, & T. A. Wongprasert (Eds.), *Avoiding Communication: Shyness, Reticence, and Communication Apprehension* (pp. 97-129). Cresskill, NJ: Hampton Press.

McCroskey, J. C. (2000). *An introduction to rhetorical communication* (8th ed.). Englewood Cliffs, NJ: Prentice Hall.

McCroskey, J. C., Ralph, D. C., & Barrick, J. E. (1970). The effect of systematic desensitization on speech anxiety. *Speech Teacher, 19,* 32–36.

McCullough, S. C., Russell, S. G., Behnke, R. R., Sawyer, C. R., & Witt, P. L. (2006). Anticipatory public speaking state anxiety as a function of body sensations and state of mind. *Communication Quarterly, 54,* 101-109.

McKay, M., Davis, M., Davis, M., Eshelman, E., Fanning, P. (2008). *The relaxation and stress workbook, 6th ed.* Oakland, CA: New Harbinger Publications.

Meichenbaum, D. (1977). *Cognitive-behavior modification.* New York: Plenum.

Motley, M. T. (1990). Public speaking anxiety qua performance anxiety: A revised model and an alternative therapy. *Journal of Social Behavior and Personality, 5*, 85–104.

Motley, M. T. (1991). Public speaking anxiety qua performance anxiety: A revised model and an alternative therapy. In M. Booth-Butterfield (Ed.) *Communication, cognition, and anxiety.* Newbury Park, CA: Sage.

Motley, M. T. (2009). COM Therapy. In J.A. Daly, J.C. McCroskey, J. Ayres, T. Hopf, D. Sonandre, & T. A. Wongprasert (Eds.), *Avoiding Communication: Shyness, Reticence, and Communication Apprehension* (pp. 337-358). Cresskill, NJ: Hampton Press.

Motley, M. T. (1998). *Overcoming your fear of public speaking--A proven method.* New York: McGraw-Hill Inc.

Motley, M., & Molloy, J. (1994). An efficacy test of a new therapy ("Communication-Orientation Motivation") for public speaking anxiety. *Journal of Social Behavior and Personality, 22*,48–58.

Mulac, A., & Sherman, A. R. (1974*). Behavioral assessment of speech anxiety. Quarterly Journal of Speech, 60*(2), 134-143.

Mulac, A., Wiemann, J. M., Moloney, E. E., & Marlow, M. L. (2009). Behavioral assessment. In J.A. Daly, J.C. McCroskey, J. Ayres, T. Hopf, D. Sonandre, & T. A. Wongprasert (Eds.), *Avoiding Communication: Shyness, Reticence, and Communication Apprehension* (pp. 205-226). Cresskill, NJ: Hampton Press.

Neenan, M. , DiGiuseppe, R., & Drydan, W. (2010). *A Primer on Rational Emotive Behavior Therapy, 3rd ed.* Champaign, IL: Research Press

O'Keefe, E. (1985). Multimodal self-management: A holistic approach to teaching self-improvement. *Human Education and Development, 6,* 176–181.

Otto, J. (1990). The effects of physical exercise on psychophysiological reactions under stress. *Cognition and Emotion, 4*, 341–357.

Overholser, J. C., Norman, W. H., & Miller, I. W. (1990). Life stress and social support in depressed patients. *Behavioral Medicine, 4*, 125–131.

Paul, G. (1966). *Insight vs. desensitization in psychotherapy. Palo Alto, CA: Stanford University Press.*

Phillips, G. M. (1977). *Rhetoritherapy versus the medical model: Dealing with reticence.* Communication Education, 26, 34–43

Phillips, G. M. (1991). *Communication incompetencies.* Carbondale, IL: Southern Illinois University Press.

Post, P. G., Wrisberg, C. A., & Mullins, S. (2010). A field test of the influence of pre-game imagery on basketball free throw shooting. *Journal of Imagery Research in Sport and Physical Activity, 5* (1), 1-15.

Prisbell, M, Dwyer, K., Carlson, R., M., Bingham, S., & Cruz, A. (2009). Connected Classroom Climate and Communication in the Basic Course: Associations with Learning. Basic Communication Course Annual 21, 161-172.

Pucel, J., & Stocker, G. (1983). A nonverbal approach to communication: A cross-cultural study of stress behaviors. *Communication, 12,* 53–65.

Ray, E. B., & Miller, K. I. (1994). Social support, home/work stress, and burnout: Who can help? *Journal of Applied Behavioral Science, 30,* 357–373.

Rice, P. L. (1987, 1998). *Stress and Health.* Pacific Grove, CA: Brooks/Cole Publishing Company.

Richmond, V., & McCroskey, J. C. (1998). *Communication: Apprehension, avoidance, and effectiveness (4th ed.).* Scottsdale, AZ: Gorsuch Scarisbrick.

Rossi, A. M., & Seiler, W. J. (1989). The comparative effectiveness of systematic desensitization and an integrative approach to treating public speaking anxiety. *Imagination, Cognition, and Personality, 9,* 49–66.

Rubin, R. B., Rubin, A. M., & Jordan, F. F. (1997). Effects of instruction on communication apprehension and communication competence. *Communication Education, 46,* 104–114.

Sachs, M. L. (1982). Exercise and running: Effects on anxiety, depression, and psychology. *Humanistic Education and Development, 21,* 51–57.

Sawyer, C. R., & Behnke, R. R. (1996). Public speaking anxiety and the communication of emotion. *World Communication, 25,* 21-30.

Sawyer, C. R., & Behnke, R. R. (1997). Communication apprehension and implicit memories of public speaking state anxiety. *Communication Quarterly, 45,* 211-222.

Sawyer, C. R., & Behnke, R. R. (1999). State anxiety patterns for public speaking and the behavior inhibition system. *Communication Reports, 12*, 33-41.

Sawyer, C. R., & Behnke, R. R. (2002). Reduction in public speaking state anxiety during performance as a function of sensitization processes. *Communication Quarterly, 50*, 110-121.

Schwartz, S. G., & Kaloupek, D. G. (1987). Acute exercise combines with imaginable exposure as a technique for anxiety reduction. *Canadian Journal of Behavioral Science, 19,* 151–166.

Seaward, B. L. (1998, 2011). *Managing stress: Principles and strategies for health and well-being.* Burlington, MA: Jones & Bartlett.

Sedlock, D., & Duda, J. (1994). The effect of trait anxiety and fitness level on heart rate and state anxiety responses to mental arithmetic stressor among college-age women. International *Journal of Sports Psychology, 25*, 218–229.

Seligmann, J., & Peyser, M. (1994). Drowning on dry land. Newsweek, 123, 64–66.

Simpson, B. A. (1982). The role of perceived self-efficacy in three treatments of speech anxiety. *Dissertation Abstracts International, 42,* 4590-B. (University Microfilms No. 8209222.)

Smith, C. D., Sawyer, C. R., & Behnke, R. R. (2005). Physical symptoms of discomfort associated with worry about giving a public speech. Communication Reports, 18, 31-41.

Smith, T. E., & Frymier, A. B. (2006). Get 'real': Does practicing speeches before an audience improve performance? *Communication Quarterly, 54,* 111-125.

Speech Communication Association (1973, December). Fears. Spectra, 9 (6), p. 4. (Article is based on The Bruskin Report, October, 1973).

Stone, W. J. (1987). *Adult fitness programs: Planning, designing, managing, and improving fitness programs.* Glenview, IL: Scott Foresman.

Thomas, J.T., Dwyer, K. & Rose, R. (2001, November). *Communication apprehension and exercise adherence: There is a relationship.* Paper presented at the annual meeting of the National Communication Association, Atlanta, GA.

U.S. Department of Health and Human Services. (1996). *Physical activity and health: A report of the Surgeon General.* Atlanta, GA: U.S. Department of Health and Human Services, Centers for Disease Control and Prevention, National Centers for Chronic Disease Prevention and Health Promotion.

U.S. Department of Health and Human Services (2010, January). *The Surgeon General's Vision for a Healthy and Fit Nation*. Rockville, MD: U.S. Department of Health and Human Services, Office of the Surgeon General.

Ullrich, P. M. & Lutgendorf, S. K. (2002). Journaling about stressful events: Effects of cognitive processing and emotional expression. *Annals of Behaviors Medicine, 24* (3), 244–250.

Van Kleeck, A., & Daly, J. A. (1982). Instructional communication research and theory: Communication development and instructional communication--A review. In Burgoon (Ed.), *Communication yearbook 5* (pp.685–715).New Brunswick, NJ: Transaction Books.

Vano, A. M. (2002). Linguistic predictors of treatment success among female substance abusers. *Dissertation Abstracts International, 62 (*12-B). (University Microfilms No. AA13036603)

Vassilopoulous, S. (2005). Social anxiety and the effects of engaging in mental imagery. *Cognitive Therapy and Research, 29*, 261_277.

Vealey, R. S., & Greenleaf, C. A. (2010). Seeing is believing: Understanding and using imagery in sport. In J. M. Williams (Ed.), *Applied sport psychology: Personal growth to peak performance* (pp. 267-304). New York: McGraw-Hill.

Waldeck, J. H., Kearney, P., & Plax, T. G. (2001). Instructional and developmental communication theory and research in the 1990s: Extending the agenda for the 21st century. In W. B. Gudykunst (Ed.), *Communication Yearbook, 24* (pp. 207-229). Thousand Oaks, CA: Sage.

Wassmer, A. E (1990). *Making contact*. New York: Henry Holt.

Watts, F. (1979). Habituation model of systematic desensitization. *Psychological Bulletin, 86*, 627–637.

Whitworth, R. H., & Cochran, C. (1996). Evaluation of integrated versus unitary treatments for reducing public speaking anxiety. *Communication Education, 45*, 306–314.

Winters, J. J., Horvath, N. R., Moss, M. N., Yarhouse, K., Sawyer, C. R., & Behnke, R. R. (2007). Affect intensity of student speakers as a predictor of anticipatory public speaking anxiety. *Texas Speech Communication Journal, 31*, 44-48.

Witt, P. L., & Behnke, R. R. (2006). Anticipatory speech anxiety as a function of public speaking assignment type. *Communication Education, 55,* 167-177.

Witt, P. L., Brown, K. C., Roberts, J. B., Weisel, J., Sawyer, C. R., & Behnke, R. R. (2006). Somatic anxiety patterns before, during, and after giving a public speech. Southern *Communication Journal, 71*, 87-100.

Wolpe, J. (1958). *Psychotherapy by reciprocal inhibition.* Palo Alto, CA: Stanford University Press.

Yates, A. (1975). *Theory and practice in behavior therapy.* New York: John Wiley.

Made in the USA
Charleston, SC
20 September 2012